CHRIST                                                    ARD

)an

# ADVANCED STUDY SKILLS

## a student's survival guide

3rd edition

# SEN Marketing

www.senbooks.co.uk

SEN Marketing
618 Leeds Road,
Outwood
Wakefield        WF1 2LT
Tel/FAX: 01924 871697

**ISBN 978 1903842 10 2**

First published in the United Kingdom, 2001.
Revised Edition 2006
Second Edition 2009
Third Edition 2012

**TRADEMARKS**

Mind-Map - is a registered trademark of Buzan Centres Ltd.
Sellotape - is a registered trademark of the Sellotape Company.
Post-it - is a registered trademark of the 3M Company.
Filofax - is a registered trademark of Filofax Group Limited.
Franklin - is the registered trademark of Franklin Electronic Publishers Ltd.
Word - is a registered trademark of Microsoft.
Read&Write GOLD - is a trademark of Texthelp Ltd

*For Christopher, who taught us both so much.*

## ACKNOWLEDGEMENTS

Our thanks go to
 David Carr for his illustrations;
 Hilary Sutton and Jo Woods for additional information;
 Linda Levett for her help and suggestions;
 former pupils, Elisabeth von Mirbach-Haff and Jonathan Mudd;
 Stephen Ostler, for his assistance with editing.

C.A.O.<br>F.A.W.

# CONTENTS

# CHAPTER 1

# INTRODUCTION TO ADVANCED STUDY SKILLS

- **What are the new demands?**
- **How to gain control**
- **Be organised**
- **Know yourself**

As you progress through the education system, you will be required to employ an increasing range of study skills and to work more independently. You will be encouraged to take responsibility for your studies and to identify your own strengths and weaknesses. Teachers will expect you to think for yourself, to take the initiative in pursuing your studies, to be self-motivated and to manage your own time effectively. In other words, you will be expected to be an independent learner.

If you can achieve this, you will be well prepared for the demands of higher education (university, apprenticeships, etc.) and the world of work.

## WHAT ARE THE NEW DEMANDS?

Key Stage 4 and Key Stage 5 courses require you to work at increasing depth, assignments become longer and require more substance. You are required to include more of your own ideas, observations or hypotheses, and to justify and explain these in detail. If you are to obtain high grades, you will need to do much reading around the subject in addition to your regular workload.

Whether you are following linear (end-of-course) or modular assessed (staged) courses, it is important to keep up with all these demands. Some courses, such as Art or Photography, require a high level of organisational skills and good time management if portfolios are to be built up systematically and assessment deadlines met.

The collection of data involves so much more than taking notes in class and reading the set text. You are required to engage with industry, the commercial world, service industries and many other types of workplace. Surveys and questionnaires are carried out and the results scrutinised and evaluated, and recorded in various formats.

## NOT SEEING THE WOOD FOR THE TREES!

It can take some time to adjust to the different approach to study required at advanced level and it is not unusual for some students to feel overwhelmed by a new subject. This reaction can be caused by the apparent size and content of the syllabus. If a number of complex topics have been introduced in quick succession it is understandable if you feel that you will never be able to get to grips with everything. It is important to appreciate that it is often necessary to start a course in this way, that is, to be introduced to a number of different issues, theories or concepts simultaneously. With time and practice, everything should fall into place and become clear.

## HALF-TERM PANIC!

In many subjects, the transition from one Key Stage (KS) to the next can be huge, especially the move from KS4 to KS5, even if you have previously achieved high grades. The demands and work approach can be very different and teachers seem to expect so much. Often you may wonder if you are going to be able to cope and may think that you have chosen the wrong subjects. The best advice is DON'T PANIC! but analyse what is worrying you, and try some of the approaches and strategies that are suggested in this book. Above all, don't keep your concerns to yourself. Talk to your tutor, teachers or friends, and work out an action plan.

## HOW TO GAIN CONTROL

Try analysing your concerns by writing down answers to these questions:

1. What worries you most? (Be specific e.g. 'I find taking notes difficult', 'I can't find my way around the library'.)

..................................................................................................

..................................................................................................

2. Do any of your fellow students have the same difficulties?  .....................
   What have they done about it?

..................................................................................................

..................................................................................................

3. Who can you approach to discuss these difficulties (teacher, tutor, friends)?

..................................................................................................

..................................................................................................

4. After discussing your concern/s with your friends and teachers, identify a strategy/strategies for coping.

..................................................................................................

..................................................................................................

Having an overview of your course can help you to feel more in control.

- Obtain a copy of the syllabus from your teacher
- List the main topics
- Find out when each topic/assignment is to be covered
- Find out when each topic/assignment is to be assessed
- Transfer the last two pieces of information to a year planner
- Find out how each topic/assignment is to be assessed (coursework, modular exam, included in a portfolio)

3

Some students find transferring the information to a Mind-Map[1] gives them an 'at-a-glance' overview of the subject on one sheet of paper. The task needs to be carried out with the help of the subject teacher/s as often choices have to be made within a set syllabus. Below is one such Mind-Map for an A level Economics course.

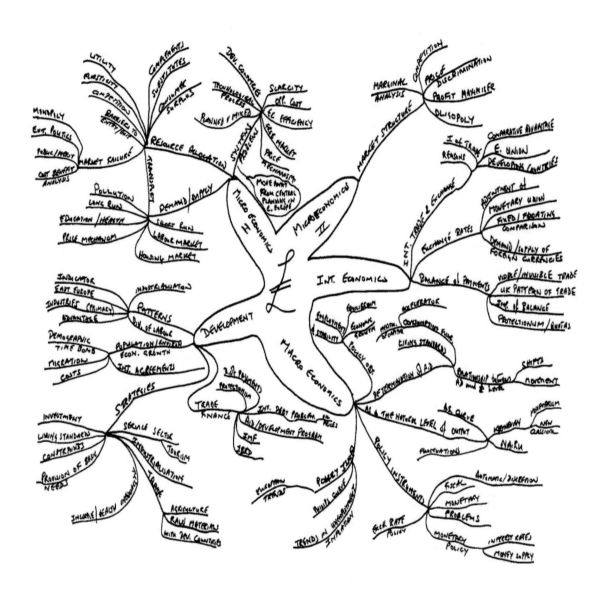

*One student made this Mind-Map so that she had an overview of her Economics course. She found it particularly helpful when she came to revise for her final examinations as she could monitor what she had covered and what remained to be revised.*

[1] Buzan, Tony, *Use Your Head*, BBC Publications, London (1979).

## BE ORGANISED

In order to cope with the increase in your workload, it is important to be organised in the allocation of your time and your work habits. See Chapter 3, *Organisation and Time Management* for suggestions and strategies.

## HAVE A GOAL

Self-motivation is one of the most important spurs to learning. Having a reason for sitting at a table, writing an essay or compiling a graph on the computer, when you would rather be watching television or out with friends, will help you to keep focused. It may be a short-term goal, e.g. maximising your coursework grade as you know you don't perform so well in written examinations, or a long-term goal, e.g. you want to get a place at a particular university in order to 'achieve a good degree so that you can work in astrophysics'. The essay or graph will be a means to an end – not always an enjoyable task, but necessary in order to reach your goal. When the going gets tough it can be helpful to pin up near where you are working a picture or quotation that sums up your goal.

## ENJOY YOUR STUDIES

Better still, if you enjoy what you are studying, it is much easier to find the motivation to get started. Try to find some aspect of the course in which you can become fully absorbed. Identify your preferred learning style and adapt it to suit the subject and task.

## KNOW YOURSELF

To be a successful student and achieve your potential you need to be able to:
- feel in control of your studies (Chapters 3, 9, 10, 11)
- recognise your preferred learning style (Chapter 2)
- maximise your learning potential (Chapters 4, 5, 6, 9)
- organise your time and work habits (Chapters 3, 7, 8)
- understand what is being asked of you (Chapters 4, 10)
- express your ideas clearly and appropriately (Chapter 6)
- give of your best in your coursework/portfolio and examinations (Chapters 7, 8, 10)
- plan for the future (Chapter 12)

We hope that this book will help you to achieve these goals. Good luck!

# CHAPTER 2

# MEMORY AND LEARNING

- **Short term v. long term memory**
- **Remembering and forgetting**
- **Learning styles questionnaire**
- **Learning style v. teaching style**

To be a successful student you will find it helpful to understand something of how memory works and why it is easier to learn and remember some things and not others.

## SHORT-TERM WORKING MEMORY

Some information is kept in the memory for a very short time. When storing a new number on your phone, you only need to retain the number long enough to punch it in. The information has stayed in your memory for just a few seconds. Other information may stay in your memory a little longer, for instance, learning for a test on the following day. You may remember the information long enough for the test, but if you were to be re-tested a month later without having reviewed the information in the meantime, your score might well be much lower. It is probable that you would have forgotten 80% of the detail.[2]

## LONG-TERM MEMORY

We can remember other information for a long time, sometimes for a lifetime. It is very likely that you can remember where you went on holiday when you were seven years old, the words to a song that you learned when you were ten, and how to swim, even if you haven't been swimming for the past three years.

## REMEMBERING

Why is it that we can remember some things with so little effort and other information will not stick? Let us examine the examples above.

[2] Buzan, Tony, *Use Your Head*, BBC Publications, London (1979).

### • The holiday

Your memory of a particular holiday is likely to be charged with strong emotions and sensory impressions – sights, sounds, smells, tastes and feelings. You may have swum without armbands for the first time, climbed a mountain, eaten octopus. These new experiences would have made a lasting impression. Embarrassing situations may also be remembered for many years, even when we would rather forget them. It seems that our feelings may play a major part where memory is concerned. This is not difficult to understand as, if we have particularly enjoyed or hated an experience, we are likely to have thought about it and talked about it, often for some time after the event. This is a form of reviewing which is very important when trying to store information in long-term memory.

### • The song

This may well have been written in rhyme and you will have heard it and sung along to it many times. The rhyme, tune and repetition will have helped the song to enter your long-term memory.

### • Swimming

The knowledge of how to swim or, for that matter, any kind of physical activity such as riding a bicycle, skiing, handwriting or playing a musical instrument, is stored in our motor memory, that is, the part of the brain which tells our muscles what to do. Motor skills have to be practised many times if they are to become automatic. Regular practice, to the point of overlearning, is essential for long-term storage. Overlearning occurs when we continue to practise or review something after we have reached mastery of the skill or topic. Once stored, it is usually possible to reactivate the skill even if it has not been practised for some years.

### • Hobbies/personal interests

Many people find that they have little difficulty remembering certain types of information: it may be the titles of all the albums recorded by their favourite group or the World Cup winners for the past twenty years. Why can we remember these details so easily? The simple answer is 'interest'. It is much easier to remember information if we are interested in the topic. We also make linkages – when we are knowledgeable about a subject we can appreciate how new information links up with our existing knowledge. We are able to categorise the new information and add it to existing memory 'hooks' because we understand its relevance. If we are interested in a subject we do not find it difficult to concentrate and so we spend time pursuing our interest.

## FORGETTING

It is not difficult to realise that information that does not seem relevant, does not interest us, that makes no impact and is not re-visited often will be soon forgotten. If new information is not reviewed within twenty-four hours, possibly 80% will be forgotten. However, even a quick read-through of the notes made in a lesson will be sufficient to bring recall of that topic back to 100%, providing the review takes place no longer than a day later. Again, some of this information will be forgotten over the next few days, but if the information is reviewed after a week, a month and then three months later, it is possible to store most of the topic in long-term memory.

## LEARNING

At this point, you may find it interesting to complete the following Learning Styles Questionnaire. Most people learn by a mixture of looking, listening, speaking and doing. However, you may have a preference for one of these modalities[3] and rely on it more than the others. It is important that you are aware of this as there may be times, perhaps when you are struggling with a specific topic, or when you switch-off during a particular teacher's lesson, when you may want to adjust your learning style to maximise your learning potential. The questionnaire is designed to give only an indication of your learning preferences. However, it can be very helpful to give some thought to the way that you prefer to work if you are to work efficiently, and there may be benefits from trying out different ways of studying.

---

[3] Senses used for perception, e.g. hearing, seeing.

# LEARNING STYLES QUESTIONNAIRE

Complete the following questions by numbering the options in your order of preference, giving 1 to the response you would make most often and 4 to the response you would make least often.

**1. You want to preset the DVD recorder in order to watch a programme later. To find out what to do would you?**

- consult the manual ☐ ♦

- get someone to tell you ☐ ♣

- watch someone else do it ☐ ♠

- work it out by trial and error ☐ ♥

**2. You are cooking a supper dish for the first time. Do you?**

- follow a recipe from a book ☐ ♦

- follow a step-by-step guide with pictures ☐ ♠

- improvise with lots of tasting ☐ ♥

- ask Mum or Dad for some instructions ☐ ♣

## 3. How do you decide what to wear on a Saturday night? Do you?

- not really think about it ♣
- put fashion before comfort ♦
- try to create an individual look ♠
- put comfort before fashion ♥

## 4. You ask someone for directions in the street. Do you?

- jot down what they say in order ♦
- visualise the route/landmarks in your mind ♠
- watch where the person is pointing ♥
- repeat the instructions several times to yourself ♣

## 5. How do you record information in a lesson or a lecture? Do you?

- just listen ♣
- create a Mind-Map ♠
- write down the information as numbered points ♦
- have difficulty because your mind keeps wandering ♥

**6. When learning how to spell new terminology in your course subject, do you?**

- just look at the word ◻ ♦

- say the word clearly to yourself
  (possibly breaking it down into syllables) ◻ ♣

- write the word out ◻ ♥

- write the word out, highlighting the difficult bits ◻ ♠

**7. You've just read a paragraph from a textbook which you haven't understood. Do you?**

- read it again and highlight the key words ◻ ♠

- read it aloud ◻ ♣

- write out the main points in order ◻ ♦

- rewrite the paragraph in your own words ◻ ♥

**8. When writing an essay, do you?**

- plan it out first making a list of the main points ◻ ♦

- plan it beforehand using a spidergram or Mind-Map ◻ ♠

- plan it in your head as you write ◻ ♣

- write it out in rough without planning and redraft it ◻ ♥

**9. Do you use any of the following methods of revising?**

- copy out your notes and diagrams ☐ ♥
- record your notes onto a digital voice recorder ☐ ♣
- draw diagrams, cartoons and/or Mind-Maps ☐ ♠
- summarise your longer notes into shorter notes ☐ ♦

**10. You have a problem when studying and you are trying to solve it. At the same time are you more likely to?**

- doodle ☐ ♠
- chew your pen ☐ ♥
- talk to yourself ☐ ♣
- stare into space ☐ ♦

**Fill in your scores for each question and the total for each row.**

| Question | 1 | 2 | 3 | 4 | 5 | 6 | 7 | 8 | 9 | 10 | Total |
|----------|---|---|---|---|---|---|---|---|---|----|-------|
| ♦ | | | | | | | | | | | |
| ♠ | | | | | | | | | | | |
| ♣ | | | | | | | | | | | |
| ♥ | | | | | | | | | | | |

**The lowest total indicates your preferred learning style.**

♦ If your lowest score is for diamonds your preferred learning style is visual and you are likely to be systematic and well organised.

♠ If your lowest score is for spades you are also a visual learner but you prefer to use pictures, diagrams and colour to record information.

♣ If your lowest score is for clubs you are an auditory learner which means that you remember most from what you hear, such as a teacher's or your own voice.

♥ If your lowest score is for hearts you are a kinaesthetic learner which means that you learn best by doing things. You are a practical, hands-on person.

## QUESTIONNAIRE IMPLICATIONS

If you do not have an obvious preference then the chances are that you are using a combination of learning styles. This is the most effective way to study because it means you can switch from one style to another, depending on what you are doing, and can benefit from whatever teaching style your teachers have. If, however, you showed a strong preference for one of the modalities, you may need to consider how successful you are as a learner, and whether you find some of your teachers easier to follow than others.

## TEACHING STYLES

In the same way that learners may have a preferred learning style and rely heavily on one or two modalities, a teacher's teaching style may be influenced by their own preferred mode[4] of learning. If your teacher's teaching style matches your preferred learning style, all will probably go well, but if there is a mismatch you may find it difficult to maintain concentration. Consequently, it can be helpful to be aware of such a possibility so that you can take compensatory action.

### ♦ The visual-systematic teacher (left-brain bias)

S/he will probably write notes on the board for you to copy, often in continuous prose, and sometimes with numbered points. Note-making from text books and essay writing will form an important part of the lessons and follow-up.

---

[4] The way something is done or experienced.

### ♠ The visual-symbolic teacher (right-brain bias)

Much of the delivery will be via a board, but this time it will involve more diagrams, flow charts, Mind-Maps, drawings and colour. It is probable that audio-visual aids will be used. Students will be expected to record their own work using similar symbolic formats.

### ♣ The auditory/oral teacher

Much of this teacher's delivery will be through the spoken word. S/he will either dictate notes or will expect the students to take notes. Oral questions and answers and discussion will form an important part of the lessons.

### ♥ The kinaesthetic teacher

The expectation of the kinaesthetic teacher will be for students to be totally involved in the lesson in a practical way. This approach is most commonly found in the Arts, Drama, P.E. and laboratory work.

## COMPENSATING FOR DIFFERENT TEACHING/LEARNING STYLES

Many teachers will draw on some or all of these approaches to accommodate the various learning preferences of their students. If you find that your teachers do not, and that during some lessons your concentration wavers, you will need to take compensatory action. For example, if your teacher is talking throughout the lesson, but you prefer a more visual approach, you will need to take notes or Mind-Map in order to sustain your concentration. If most of the lesson is spent copying notes from the board and you are an aural/oral learner, you will need to read your notes aloud shortly after the lesson and discuss the contents with your fellow students. If you don't, it is likely that you will assimilate very little from that lesson.

## SUMMARY

In order to learn and remember information it is necessary that some of the following elements are present – the more the better:

- **Interest**
- **Understanding**
- **Concentration**
- **Linkages**
- **Repetition/practice**
- **Emotional impact**
- **Rhyme/melody**
- **Knowledge of your preferred learning style**
- **Awareness of your teachers' preferred teaching styles**

These key elements will be considered further in Chapter 9, *Revision* and in Chapter 10, *Examinations*.

# CHAPTER 3

# ORGANISATION AND TIME MANAGEMENT

- **Motivation**
- **A place to work**
- **Keeping notes organised**
- **Having the right equipment**
- **Meeting deadlines**
- **Concentrating**
- **Music**
- **Using time wisely**
- **Getting down to work**

Many students admit to having difficulties in these areas. They know what they should be doing, but have difficulty motivating themselves to get organised and to get started. So what needs to be done?

## MOTIVATION

Hopefully, there will be aspects of your courses that you will enjoy for their own sake and so you will not need external incentives to motivate you to study. However, for the times when this is not the case you will need to remind yourself of a good reason for getting on with your work. It can be helpful to have both short-term and long-term goals. The long-term goal may well be the qualifications you need to reach the next step in your education, or you may have a particular career in mind for which you need certain qualifications. A short-term goal may be to complete a piece of coursework so that you are free to go out at the weekend.

## A PLACE TO WORK

Psychologically, it is helpful to have a regular place that you associate with working. This may be a desk in your bedroom, a work-bay in your school library or the quiet room in a public library. If you are fortunate enough to have your own workspace you are at a great advantage as you can arrange it so that everything is to hand.

### User-friendly furniture
It is usually assumed that students work best at a desk or table, although some students do manage to work sitting on their bed or floor. The important thing is

*Organisational Skills*

to assess, from time-to-time, whether you are working at maximum efficiency, or whether your handwriting is suffering because you are not working on a firm surface, your back is aching because your chair is the wrong height for the table, you are too hot/cold, the light is inadequate and so on.

Writing on a sloping surface, which can be improvised from a piece of chipboard, can alleviate neck and back problems caused by leaning over a desk for too long; a cushion on your chair or books under the legs of your table can help achieve the appropriate height for the two pieces of furniture, and an adjustable desk lamp can allow you to direct the light so that you are not working in shadow. Some students find the natural light from a window kinder on the eyes than fluorescent tubes, whilst others find the view from a window too distracting. Be honest with yourself and try different arrangements to see what really suits you best.

## KEEPING NOTES ORGANIZED

### 1. Files
Ensure, right from the beginning of a course, that you have separate files for each subject and that you label file dividers for each new topic as it is introduced. This seems too obvious to mention, but it is very easy to put off the filing of notes until later, only to find that when they are needed for revision purposes they have gone missing. To avoid sheets of file paper becoming lost, keep a packet of hole reinforcers in your pencil case for use as soon as a hole rips.

### 2. Handouts
If you are given handouts that are not already hole-punched, you need to keep handy either a hole-punch, or some plastic wallets into which to slip them, as handouts get lost or crumpled very easily if they are not filed immediately.

### 3. Expanding files
An expanding file with pockets and a solid spine, resembling an arch-lever file when stood on end, can be used for storing paperwork that will not fit into your files, or is not subject-specific. Each section can be labelled with a Post-it note and easily relabelled when necessary. This is an organisational strategy aimed at avoiding panic when you are searching for a particular piece of paper, handout, newspaper cutting, brochure, etc.

### 4. Magazine holders
A number of subjects, especially Geography, Economics, Business Studies and Leisure and Tourism have supporting reading matter in the form of magazines. These can be kept in plastic or reinforced cardboard magazine holders, preferably on a shelf near where you normally work. If you use Post-it notes to mark the pages of particularly useful articles, much time can be saved when researching a project.

# HAVING THE RIGHT EQUIPMENT

It will help you to get started if you have everything to hand. Here are a few suggestions. You will need to add your own subject-specific items.

| | **Additional items** |
|---|---|
| Paper: lined/graph/tracing/drawing | |
| Plastic wallets/files/folders | ................................. |
| Fountain pen/Biros/coloured pens | ................................. |
| Highlighters | ................................. |
| Pencils of various hardness | ................................. |
| Eraser/correction fluid | ................................. |
| Pencil sharpener | ................................. |
| Maths set | ................................. |
| Calculator | ................................. |
| Ruler | ................................. |
| Hole reinforcers | ................................. |
| Hole punch | ................................. |
| Scissors | ................................. |
| Sellotape | ................................. |
| Paper clips | ................................. |
| Stapler & staples | ................................. |
| Glue stick | ................................. |
| Post-it notes | ................................. |
| Dictionary for definitions | ................................. |
| Electronic spell checker for spellings | ................................. |
| Thesaurus to give variety to your vocabulary | ................................. |

For suggestions regarding ICT equipment see Chapter 8, *Information and Communication Technology*.

# MEETING DEADLINES

Many students comment that developing good time management is probably the hardest aspect of study skills. This problem can be tackled under three headings: Yearly planning, Weekly planning and Daily planning.

## Yearly planning

At the beginning of the academic year it can be useful to fill in a year planner to be pinned on the wall. This will give you an overview of the year to come and will help you plan for long-term deadlines. Large calendar formats can be obtained from office supply retailers, or bought in bulk (this is a cheaper option for schools and colleges). An A4 format is included in *Appendix 5* and may be photocopied. Electronic calendars with reminders can also be created on a computer or a mobile phone.

The following can be entered on the planner:

- Holidays
- Field trips
- Modular and end-of-year examinations
- Coursework deadlines
- Careers conventions, university/college open days & other events that will affect normal lessons and private study

Different coloured highlighters can be used for each category. You will then have an at-a-glance record of what is coming up and this will be particularly useful when planning your revision programme.

## Weekly planning

You will already have a timetable of your lessons or lectures. It can be helpful to have a fresh copy for each week with blank boxes for study periods. This will enable you to plan ahead with regard to how you are going to use your free periods. It is very easy to waste precious time if at the beginning of a study period you have no idea what you are going to do. However, if at the beginning of the week you can anticipate what research, reading around the subject, writing up of notes, essay planning, graphs and drawings you will need to do, you can then allocate various tasks to various days. If your entries are written in pencil, it is easy enough to change them if your priorities change. A diary or personal organiser can be used in place of a timetable if preferred. Many schools supply custom-made homework diaries which contain columns for filling in 'date-due' and for ticking off when work is handed in. A weekly timetable is included in *Appendix 5*, which may be photocopied. It can be made larger or smaller to suit your particular needs.

## Daily planning

To help foster a feeling of being in control of your studies, it is worth spending a few moments first thing in the morning thinking through the day ahead and setting yourself a specific objective in addition to the usual routine of lessons and study periods. This could be a visit to the library to find supplementary reading material for a project, speaking to your tutor about a particular concern, or making a plan for a piece of coursework. Hopefully, at the end of the day, an appraisal of how successful you have been in reaching your objective will help you feel that you are making progress. If, however, you did not achieve your objective, do not allow it to make you give up on your studies, but set yourself a more manageable task for the next day.

## CONCENTRATING

'More' does not necessarily equal 'better'. It is not an unusual experience for a student to sit reading for two hours, only to realise that for the second hour nothing sank in. One hour of well-focused reading can be far more valuable than two hours of staring at a book aimlessly (see Chapter 4, *Reading and Understanding*).

Each of us has our own optimum concentration span. It may vary according to the activity or subject. You may be only too aware that your concentration wavers. The important thing is to do something about it when you find yourself fidgeting, looking out of the window or wondering what you are reading about. It is worth trying one or more of the following suggestions. Obviously, your actions will be governed by whether you are at home, in a library or in a lesson.

- Have a short break; move about; make a drink; get some fresh air
- Switch from reading to note-making
- Highlight key words
- Use coloured pens in your note-making
- Convert linear[5] notes into a Mind-Map
- Tape-record notes
- Have a question-and-answer session with a friend
- Explain what you have been studying to someone else
- Start working on another subject

[5] Using lines: linear notes are written one under another, down a page.

## MUSIC

Opinion is divided over whether listening to music while you are working is a help or a hindrance.

### Arguments against

- It is a distraction and will slow you down
- If it does not slow you down, you can't be listening to it, so there is no point in having it on.

### Arguments in favour

- It blots out other noises that are more distracting
- It is like a comforting blanket
- It stops you getting bored
- It aids concentration

### Other considerations

If you do listen to music take note of whether you work more efficiently when listening to instrumental tracks, with no lyrics. Words can sometimes interfere with language processing. There is evidence that listening to music which has a regular rhythm similar to your heart beat, that is predictable with a forward pulling motion and with no surprises, can stimulate at an appropriate level and can aid concentration. Certain works by Mozart and Bach are particularly suitable. Modern music rarely fulfils all the criteria. The most important consideration is: Does it work for you?


## USING TIME WISELY

All students have good days and bad days with respect to how much they manage to achieve. The following suggestions might be helpful when attempting to use time wisely:

- Keep a list of priorities – review regularly
- Plan ahead, both daily and weekly
- Set yourself targets (e.g. spend 1/2 hour making notes on a chapter)
- Monitor whether you are keeping focused or becoming side-tracked
- Recognise what tends to distract you and deal with the problem

The best way to approach the last suggestion is to build the distraction into your daily or weekly timetable. This way you won't feel deprived of the things you enjoy doing. For instance, you could telephone a friend, read a magazine, or walk the dog as a refreshing break between your work sessions. However, ensure that you build in a time limit or you might not get back to work.

# GETTING DOWN TO WORK

When taking physical exercise it is usual to have:

- A warm-up session
- A strenuous activity
- A cool-down session

This way you can maximise your physical potential without too much fear of injury. A study session can be tackled in the same way.

## Warm-up

- Ensure that you have all the resources you will need to hand
- Read through the instructions/assignment
- Refresh your memory regarding the topic by reading through your notes, looking at examples, linking with related topics

You should now be ready to get started.

## Strenuous activity

Having warmed-up and focused your attention on the task in hand, you can now tackle the main assignment, be it making notes on a new topic, planning or writing an essay, working through an exercise, or solving a problem. Continue until you feel that your concentration is wavering, or five minutes before the end of a fixed private study period.

## Cool-down

- Look through what you have done
- Check with the original instructions. If you have not finished, or you have gone off at a tangent that is not relevant, note what you need to do in your next work session
- Make a note of anything you did not understand
- If appropriate, write yourself questions to test your recall at a future date
- Appraise how successful the work session has been

## ORGANISATIONAL STRATEGIES

Complete these sentences:

I am going to improve my work-space by ................................................

..............................................................................................................

My notes and resources need to be ...........................................................

..............................................................................................................

I have pinned/filed my yearly, weekly and daily planners ............................

..............................................................................................................

I need a break after ...............................................................................

..............................................................................................................

I find music aids/does not aid my concentration. (delete as appropriate)

# CHAPTER 4

# READING AND UNDERSTANDING

- **Reading for different purposes**
- **Different reading techniques**
- **Overcoming difficulties with reading**
- **Understanding complex texts**
- **Interpreting essay and examination questions**

For many students one of the most daunting aspects of study at KS4 and KS5 is the amount of reading required. In order to succeed it is not only necessary to read within specific topic areas but also to read widely around the course. Teachers always stress the need for general reading. The reason for this is so that you extend your background knowledge of the subject. Sometimes it is difficult to find the time when you are taking a number of other subjects and trying to balance the demands of a social life and possibly a part-time job.

Reading is a two-way process. When we read our minds interact with the text and we draw on knowledge that we already possess to make sense of the new information. This is why reading around a subject is so important. Watching TV news and documentaries and reading a quality newspaper are also ways of extending your knowledge base.

It may help to consider how we read and for what purpose.

## READING FOR DIFFERENT PURPOSES

People read for different reasons. They may read:
- for pleasure – novels, magazines, non-fiction, poetry
- for information – bus/train timetables, recipes, menus, newspapers
- to follow instructions – DIY manuals, leaflets accompanying purchases
- to study – assignment titles, essay questions, research, general reading

## DIFFERENT READING TECHNIQUES

Even when you are reading for pleasure, you adapt your technique according to your material. For example, you do not read every word in a magazine from cover to cover. Instead you flick through the pages to find an interesting article. If your attention has been caught by one of the captions on the front cover you might use the contents page to find the page number of the relevant article and then turn straight to that page.  On the other hand, if you read a novel in the same way, you would soon lose the plot!  In order to follow the development of a novel and appreciate the way it has been written you need to read it closely from beginning to end.  Even so, you are likely to skip words or even whole paragraphs if you are reading purely for recreation.

However, if you were studying that particular novel, you would have to read it more closely, making notes as you went along on features such as characterisation and style.  You might also be advised to read other novels by the same author or by other authors from the same period in history.

Let us review these different reading techniques:

- **Recreational reading**

  This is often referred to as 'light reading'.  It does not involve recalling later what you have read although you may choose to do so.

- **Skimming**

  This involves looking quickly at a page, chapter or a whole book to get a rough idea of what it contains.  It is helpful to use the organisational features of the printed page, e.g. titles, subheadings, diagrams, illustrations, abstracts, summaries and footnotes.

- **Scanning**

  This involves looking for particular information.  You need to move your eyes quickly across the page until you locate a specific word or phrase and then read that section carefully to see if it is relevant.

- **Detailed reading**

  This involves careful word-by-word reading at normal speed.  It is necessary to read in this way in order to understand complex information once you have located it by skimming and scanning.

- **Reading for study**

  This will involve the use of skimming and scanning techniques in order to locate specific information.  You then read closely, making notes in order to recall the content later. (See Chapter 5, *Taking and Making Notes*)

# OVERCOMING DIFFICULTIES WITH READING

Many students report difficulty with detailed reading when studying. The most common problems are:

- maintaining concentration
- understanding complex texts
- reading too slowly

## Maintaining concentration

It is much easier to concentrate on detailed reading for study if you have a purpose in mind. One method is to ask yourself specific questions before you start reading to help you focus on the content. These questions may be suggested already by your assignment title or you may formulate them during the skimming and scanning processes.

## SQ3R[6]

One tried-and-tested formula for reading in this way is known as **SQ3R** which stands for **Survey – Question – Read – Recall – Review**.

## Survey

Look at the book as a whole to see whether it is what you need for your assignment. Check the title, author, blurb on the book cover, contents page, illustrations, index, chapter headings, introduction, first and last paragraphs.

## Question

Why am I reading this?
What do I know already about this topic?
Can I make links? What am I looking for?
Have I found it?
Do I need to read all of this book, or just certain chapters?

## Read

Now read the book or chapter in more detail. First skim, that is, read quickly to get an overall impression. Then scan the text for specific information. Pick out key words or phrases. Finally read slowly, highlighting or underlining important information and making notes either in the margin or on a pad. If it is a library book you can highlight a page by using a clear plastic overlay and a water soluble overhead projector pen, transferring your notes onto cards or paper at the end of each page.

[6] Robinson, Francis, *Effective Study*, 1946.

## Recall

Check that you have remembered what you have read.  Try:

- reciting aloud
- explaining it to someone else
- writing down a summary of important passages.

## Review

Go back to your notes – how much did you remember?
Go back to the original text – have you missed out anything important?
Repeat this review process before handing in your assignment or as part of your revision.

If your mind still wanders when you read try some of the following:

- Ask yourself if the text is suitable.  Perhaps it is too difficult and you should try to find something that is more accessible.  This is not defeatist– just practical.

- Make notes after reading each paragraph.

- Try reading aloud.

- Make a recording of yourself reading the text aloud.  It is easier to remember the sound of your own voice and you can listen to it whilst you are relaxing.  It will also be useful later for revision.

- If you want to record the text, but it is proving too difficult for you to read, ask someone else to read it for you.  Many literary texts are now available as audiobooks or e-books.

- Highlight key words if it is your own book.

## Understanding complex texts

If you have difficulty understanding a text, don't give up straight away. Stop and consider what might be the reason. Ask yourself these questions:

- Do I have enough background knowledge to understand what the author is talking about? (If not, try going down a level and find a book written for a previous Key Stage in order to familiarise yourself with the topic.)

- Is the vocabulary too difficult? If you do not understand technical terms, look them up and write definitions on index cards or in a small notebook for easy reference. Invest in a good dictionary that is subject-specific and keep it by you when studying.

- Am I taking the text too literally and missing the author's intention? One of the hardest aspects of reading at this level is not reading the lines of words but 'reading between the lines'. This is easier said than done! However, it is as well to be aware of some of the pitfalls of interpreting text too literally.

1. You must be able to **INFER** meaning from a text. This means that you must be able to draw out what the author intends to say beyond what is literally printed on the page. Authors often hint or suggest something without stating it directly, for example:

*"Having scrambled for a seat on the train, Kate reached for the letter which had arrived that morning. Then she remembered she had left her glasses on the kitchen table."*

We can infer from this text that Kate was not able to read the letter until she went home but the author does not have to tell us this directly.

2. You must be able to detect **BIAS**. You must not assume that all writers can be trusted as authorities in their subjects. They may well be writing from a particular point of view and you need to be aware of the distinction between fact and opinion. Many newspapers display bias, for example:

*"Villagers protest over Frankenstein crops."*

In this imaginary newspaper headline the word 'Frankenstein' is intended to sway the reader against the concept of genetically modified crops.

3. You must be aware of **METAPHOR.** Consider the following statements:

*"The building collapsed after the bomb exploded."*

*"The English cricket team collapsed just before tea."*

The first sentence means exactly what it says: the building was reduced to rubble as a consequence of the explosion. This is an example of literal meaning. The second sentence is an example of a metaphor, that is, a figure of speech in which a comparison is implied between two essentially different ideas. If you took this statement literally then you would doubtless conjure up a scene of disaster in your mind with a fleet of ambulances ferrying the English players off the pitch. However if you had some cricketing knowledge you would be aware of the sentence's metaphorical meaning. You would realise that the word 'collapsed' meant that the team was 'all out', still in good health although perhaps a little depressed at seeing their opponents coming in to bat.

4. You must be able to respond to an author's **TONE.** Much can be gained by imagining that you are listening to the author reading aloud. What tone of voice would he or she use? In particular be aware of the range of techniques used to create a humorous effect in writing. Some of these, such as irony, can be very subtle and are easily missed.

- **Irony** is shown when the author deliberately says the opposite of, or something different from, what s/he means, in order to make the real meaning more emphatic. For example, in Shakespeare's 'Julius Caesar' Mark Antony refers to Brutus as "an honourable man" after he has taken part in the murder of Caesar, thus emphasising to the crowd how *dishonourable* Brutus has been.

- **Sarcasm** often includes irony but it is not the same. It involves the use of bitter language in order to hurt or wound. For example, calling someone "clever" when they have just done something stupid makes the point in a spiteful way:

  "What a *clever* thing to do!"

- **Exaggeration** (hyperbole) is important because you have to ask yourself why the author is using such language, for example: in 'Dr Faustus' Christopher Marlowe describes Helen of Troy as "the face that launch'd a thousand ships" to emphasise her outstanding beauty. Hyperbole is often used to achieve a satirical effect.

- **Understatement** occurs when the importance or seriousness of something is reduced deliberately in order to diminish its impact, e.g. when a serious wound is dismissed as a 'mere scratch'.

- **Euphemism** is a particular kind of understatement when a harsh or unpleasant fact is expressed politely. Its use is increasing as a result of the current need for writers to observe 'political correctness'. This can sometimes contribute to the humorous effect of a passage, e.g. the use of 'vertically challenged' instead of the word 'short'.

- **Anticlimax** (bathos) is the deliberate spoiling of the build-up to a climax. It usually involves the introduction of something incongruous or unsuitable at the end of a serious list, e.g. "He fought to defend his country, his honour and his pet mouse."

## Reading too slowly

If you are a slow reader it can be very discouraging to have to wade through numerous texts before you can begin an assignment.

- Use the skimming and scanning techniques to make sure that you *need* to read everything

- Select passages for close reading carefully
- Use a finger or ruler under the line of print or down the side of the page to force your eyes to move on and not to fixate. If this makes you feel self-conscious in public, use a white index card and jot keywords on it.
- Try using a coloured plastic overlay. (Cut up a plastic document wallet)
- Practise reading faster. Set aside 15 to 20 minutes each day when you know you won't be interrupted. Using easy material to start with (newspaper or magazine articles) read each article as quickly as possible, making sure that you also understand it. Time yourself with a watch or stopwatch and work out your rate of reading in words per minute. (Estimate the number of words by multiplying the number of lines by the average number of words per line.) Keep a chart of your reading rate. As you increase in speed, progress to more difficult material, making sure you still understand what you are reading.[7]

## INTERPRETING ESSAY AND EXAMINATION QUESTIONS

In order to avoid misinterpreting essay titles and, more commonly, examination questions and instructions you must make sure that you read every word closely. Underline or highlight the key words and look for tricky words which can completely alter the meaning of a sentence, like 'not'. (It is easy to overlook small words when you are nervous.) Make sure that you write the title of the question in full at the beginning of your essay or exam answer so that you can refer back to the wording. It is a good idea to write the keywords of the question title in coloured pen to keep you focused. Discipline yourself to read the question through at least twice and return to it frequently as you write. For an explanation of some of the most common words used in essay titles see Chapter 6, *Essay Writing*.

## SUMMARY

- **Consider why you are reading a text.**
- **Focus your reading by asking questions**
- **Maintain concentration by varying reading techniques**
- **Remember to 'read between the lines' to improve understanding of complex texts**
- **Practise reading faster**

---

[7] Lunzer, E and Gardner, K (Eds.) *The Effective Use of Reading*, Schools Council Project, Heinemann Educational Books, 1979

# CHAPTER 5

# TAKING AND MAKING NOTES

- **How to take notes from speech**
- **Making notes**
- **Different note formats**
- **Organising notes**

## What is the purpose of making notes?

Note-making is an important part of studying. It enables you to engage with a text or lesson, formulate your ideas and record your thought process. In particular, note-making enables you to review a lesson and revise for exams. Unless you possess exceptional recall you would soon forget the content of a book or lecture: it is your notes which enable you to access the information and your response to it at a later stage.

There is no right way or wrong way to make notes – only the way that works for you. The method you choose to record information usually depends on your individual learning style (see Chapter 2, *Memory and Learning*).

There are two processes involved.

### 1. Taking notes

You will need to be able to take notes from speech in the form of:

- a lesson
- a lecture
- a film or video/DVD
- a radio programme or audio recording
- dictation

### 2. Making notes

You will need to make notes either before a lesson as preparation or after a lesson as a follow-up. You will be expected to make notes from:

- a handout
- a textbook
- a library book
- other research or source material
- your own lesson notes
- a practical experiment or investigation
- a visit or field trip

# HOW TO TAKE NOTES FROM SPEECH

In the sixth form you will be expected to record information in a lesson or lecture as the teacher speaks. For many students this is a difficult process, as they have not been trained to do so and find that the teacher speaks too quickly for them to write everything down. Some teachers, aware of the problem, give out interactive handouts containing the framework of the lesson so that you can focus your listening and fill in missing words or examples. Others give out the full text of a lesson or lecture; in this case it is a good idea to highlight the important points and annotate the text so that you can make your own notes later.

If your teacher has an auditory teaching style and talks throughout the lesson, expecting you to write down what s/he says, or dictates notes, you must not attempt to write down every single word, or full sentences. If you write at an average or slow speed you will find yourself missing vital pieces of information as the teacher moves on and you are still struggling to record the previous point. If you are having problems keeping up:

- Ask if you can use a voice recorder. This is a good way to record a lesson and to relieve the pressure but you should still make brief notes, as it is very time-consuming to have to play back the full recording in order to make your detailed notes.
- Jot down key words and phrases, leaving gaps to be filled in later. If necessary, borrow a friend's notes after the lesson to complete yours.
- Ask a sympathetic friend to act as your scribe and make a copy of his/her notes.

**When taking notes:**

- Write on one side of A4 paper only, giving room to expand your notes.
- Double-space lines and leave a wide margin.
- Always write the date and title at the top of the first page. (This sounds obvious but it makes filing much easier later.)
- Make sure you jot down key words and phrases.
- Leave out little words like 'the', 'a' and 'an' which don't affect the sense. Words like 'not' and 'but' are important.
- Use shorthand. You don't need to go on a course to be able to do this. Try to devise your own system of symbols and abbreviations to make writing faster but be consistent so that you can read them back.
- Go over your notes and write them up as soon as possible after a lesson or lecture.

## A list of common abbreviations and symbols

| | |
|---|---|
| e.g. | for example |
| i.e. | (Latin: id est) that is |
| etc. | (Latin: et cetera) and the rest |
| & | and |
| % | percentage |
| cf. | compare |
| no. | number |
| ch. | chapter |
| C | century |
| c. | (Latin: circa) around, about |
| + | plus |
| - | minus |
| ∧ | insert, omitted |
| ~ | approximately |
| @ | at |
| N.B. | (Latin: nota bene) note well, take note |
| < | less than |
| > | more than |
| = | equals |
| ≠ | does not equal |
| ∴ | therefore |
| ∵ | because |
| exc. | except |
| fig. | figure |
| w/ | with |
| b4 | before |
| v. | very |
| → | leading to |
| opp. | opposite |

Try to make your own shorthand for words that occur frequently in the subjects you are studying. For example:

| | |
|---|---|
| Ren. | Renaissance |
| rsch. | research |
| invg. | investigate |
| Lit. | Literature |

# MAKING NOTES

You will also have to make notes in your own time from a variety of written sources such as:

## 1. **A handout**
Read through the text and highlight or underline the key words and main ideas. Then, without looking back at the original text, write a summary in your own words, adding your own comments or extra information.

## 2. **A textbook**
If you own the textbook you can highlight or underline freely. Try to avoid writing too many comments in the margin, as they can be distracting. If you are not supposed to mark the text you can highlight the key words using a clear plastic overlay and dry wipe marker pen. (You can cut up plastic document folders for this purpose.) Use these highlighted words as the basis of your notes.

## 3. **A library book or source material**
If it would help you to mark the text ask the librarian if you can photocopy the relevant pages in order to highlight or underline the main points on your copy before making your notes.

## 4. **Your own lesson notes**
To remember the information effectively, it is best to return to your lesson or lecture notes the same day. Research has shown that after only ten minutes your ability to recall knowledge begins to decline steeply and by the end of twenty-four hours you will have retained only 20% of the information unless you have reviewed it. (see Chapter 2, *Memory and Learning*).

It cannot be stressed too strongly how important it is to get into the habit of writing up notes on a daily basis so that you make a record of your study from which you can revise later. Although final examinations may seem a long way off, your course will pass very quickly and you may not have the time to make up your notes properly at a later date.

## 5. **A video/DVD**
If you are taking notes from a video/DVD at home then it is a good idea to watch it all the way through first before writing anything down. This will enable you to think about what you are looking for and to formulate questions to focus your viewing. You might ask yourself:

"Why am I watching this?"
"What information do I hope to find?"
"Is the presentation likely to be biased in favour of a particular point of view?"

Draw out a grid on a blank piece of paper on which you can fill in the main points or key words as you watch the video/DVD for the second time, using the pause button as necessary. Do not attempt to write long sentences.

## An example of a video/DVD grid

| MAIN POINT | SUPPORTING DETAILS |
|---|---|
| 1 | |
| 2 | |
| 3 | |
| 4 | |
| 5 | |

If you have to watch a video/DVD as part of a lesson or lecture do not spend too much time writing notes. Jot down the main points as headings and add detailed information as soon as possible after viewing, before you forget it.

## Some suggestions for writing up notes

You must experiment with different techniques and formats until you find a style of note-making which works for you. Always bear in mind why you are making notes. Some notes, such as those made as preparation for a discussion or a lesson, need less care than those which are to be used for revision. It is worth spending time on revision notes to avoid panic later.

1. **Write legibly**. If you have difficulty revising from your own handwriting, use a word-processor. This method has the added advantage of allowing you to insert more information. You can also make your own exercises for revision before your exams. (See Chapter 9, *Revision*).

2. **Make your notes visually appealing.** Leave plenty of spaces and use colour whenever you can. For example, quotations can be written in a differently coloured ink.

3. **Use pictures, symbols and diagrams** to illustrate your notes. These will make them seem more personal and will help recall.

4. **Use headings, sub-headings and bullet points** when making linear notes (see the example on page 39). This will make it easier to find information and to learn from your notes.

5. **Use abbreviations** - don't write in full sentences.

6. **Use block capitals or underlining** for **key words**.

7. **Don't copy out chunks from books.** Always put notes into your own words. Write down page references and full titles of books you have used.

8. **Check spellings**, especially of technical or subject-specific vocabulary. You will be penalised for incorrect spelling of these words in the exams.

9. **Experiment with different forms of note making**. For example, try converting your linear notes into a spidergram or a Mind-Map.

10. **Make revision cards as you go along.** It is a good idea to record key facts on index cards while they are still fresh in your mind. They can be used for revision before a module or final examination. If you do this throughout your course it relieves the sense of being overwhelmed as the exams approach because you feel as if you have already made some revision progress.

## DIFFERENT NOTE FORMATS

The method and style you use to record your notes will depend on the subject matter and on your own individual learning style.

♦ If you are a visual, left-brained learner you will probably prefer notes which are systematic and sequential. You will use linear notes in the form of listed points.

♠ If you are a visual, right-brained learner you will prefer patterned notes such as a flow chart and will find colour and drawings useful.

♣ An auditory learner may need to record notes aloud using a voice recorder.

♥ A kinaesthetic learner will learn best by writing notes out several times, using different formats.

## Linear notes

These are notes written, as the name suggests, in lines. They usually consist of main headings and sub-headings. These can be made clearer by underlining, highlighting, use of colour, numbering points and using bullets.

## An example of linear notes

### TAKING AND MAKING NOTES

1. Taking notes from
   - a lesson
   - a lecture
   - a film or video/DVD
   - a radio programme or audio recording
   - dictation

2. Making notes from
   - a textbook
     highlight or underline key words
   - a handout
     make a summary in your own words
   - a library book
     photocopy
   - other research material
   - your own lesson notes
     write up daily
   - a practical experiment or investigation
   - a visit or field trip

It is a good idea to leave a wide margin on both sides of the paper and to double-space linear notes so that additional points can be added later.

## Flow Charts

Flow Charts can be used to illustrate a sequence of events or a process. Geometric shapes are linked by arrows: ovals are used for 'start' and 'finish'; diamonds to pose a question and rectangles to denote an action or a decision.

**Example of a Flow Chart – an analysis of why you may be finding a subject difficult.**

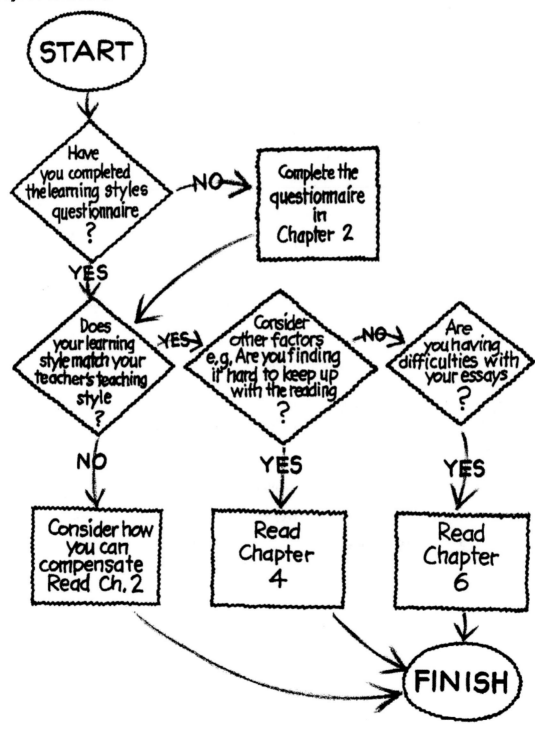

## Patterned notes

These are notes recorded in a shape or pattern. They are sometimes referred to as spidergrams, Mind-Maps or web notes. These notes rely on the imagination to link ideas by association. They consist of a central image from which branches radiate. These in turn lead into smaller branches. They are illustrated with patterns, symbols and 3-D images. Colour is used to differentiate ideas. If you are a person who works well visually then it is worth trying mind-mapping as a method of recording.

## An example of a Mind-Map.

### Revision Cards

Index cards can be stored in different coloured plastic boxes (or shoe boxes) according to subject.

### An example of a revision card

---

## Learning Styles

♦ <u>visual, left-brained learner</u> - prefers linear notes

♠ <u>visual, right-brained learner</u> - prefers patterned notes, colour and drawings

♣ <u>auditory learner</u> - may prefer to record notes aloud

♥ <u>kinaesthetic learner</u> - prefers to write out notes

---

## ORGANISING NOTES

This has been covered in Chapter 3, *Organisation and Time Management*. However, it is worth emphasising that you must file your notes on a regular basis, especially if you are transferring them from a 'working file' into a separate subject file. Use cardboard file dividers for each section and write the contents in pencil on the front of each section. This can be written in ink when the file is complete. An index at the front of the file will enable you to find topics easily. Where topics fall into more than one section of the syllabus you can mark your notes in the corner with a colour corresponding to each syllabus area.

## SUMMARY

- **Experiment with different note formats**
- **Review lesson/lecture notes on the same day**
- **Write up notes as soon as possible**
- **Make revision cards as you progress through the course**
- **File notes regularly**

# CHAPTER 6

# ESSAY WRITING

- **Interpreting the question**
- **Question words and their definitions**
- **Organisation of ideas**
- **The stages of writing**
- **Writing clearly**

"I have all the ideas in my head but they won't go down my arm and onto the paper." (A Level Theatre Studies Student)

This sense of frustration is common amongst students who have to write essays as part of their course or in examinations. There are three main problem areas:

- **interpreting** the question
- **organising** the main ideas into essay form
- **writing** clearly and concisely in fluent English

## INTERPRETING THE QUESTION

Students often lose marks for their essays because they either misinterpret the question or do not answer it correctly. A common mistake is to write down everything, instead of selecting the information that is relevant to the question. One of the hardest things is knowing what to include and what to leave out.

When you are given an essay question, always highlight or underline the key words. Never lose sight of the question. Keep referring to the key words throughout your essay. Then, in your opening paragraph, you should demonstrate that you have understood the question by paraphrasing it (putting it into your own words) and explaining how you are going to answer it. Spotting what your tutor or the examiner is looking for is the key to successful essay writing.

Different subjects may require different essay techniques. There are many good subject-specific revision books now available, which will give you a detailed guide to the technique appropriate to your subject. Try the study guides published by Macmillan, Letts or Longman, which are obtainable from all good bookshops.

# QUESTION WORDS AND THEIR DEFINITIONS

| analyse | show the main ideas, how they are interrelated and why they are important |
|---|---|
| assess | describe the strengths and weaknesses; give opinions |
| compare | look for similarities and differences |
| contrast | bring out the differences |
| criticise | give your judgement or opinion of a topic, showing its good *and* bad points |
| describe | give a detailed picture in words |
| discuss | outline the details and give all sides of the argument |
| distinguish between | make clear the differences between |
| evaluate | give the advantages and disadvantages and then give your opinion |
| examine | discuss in detail and give an opinion |
| explain | make something clear and give reasons for it |
| illustrate | literally draw a diagram, picture or chart and make clear by giving examples |
| interpret | make something clear, possibly giving your opinion |
| justify | give reasons for accepting a particular opinion or statement; possibly give an argument |
| list | also 'enumerate'; give a list of items and number them |
| outline | explain the main ideas and show how they are interrelated; leave out details |
| refute | give reasons why an argument or statement is false |
| relate | show the connections between things, either causal links or similarities |
| review | give a survey or summary of a topic and your assessment of it |
| state | give the main points of a topic in clear language; omit details |
| summarise | give the main features of an argument, omitting details and examples |
| trace | follow the progress of an idea or topic either in time or through the relationship of cause and effect |

# ORGANISATION OF IDEAS

An essay is a continuous piece of writing in response to a set question. It should contain the clear development of your ideas from the introduction to the conclusion.

Your essay should be written in paragraphs. A paragraph should contain four or five sentences about a single idea. The main topic of a paragraph is usually contained in the first sentence (sometimes known as the topic sentence).

When your tutor reads the topic sentence s/he should have a clear idea of what is to follow. The rest of the paragraph should expand the main idea by giving examples, evidence or justification for the main statement. Topic sentences form the skeleton of your essay. The remaining sentences 'flesh out' your argument.

## The shape of a paragraph

| Topic sentence | | |
|---|---|---|
| Supporting sentences | a | |
| | b | |
| | c | |
| | d | |

Paragraphs should not be too long or they become unwieldy and difficult to read. You should aim to communicate your ideas as clearly and as simply as possible.

Always start a new paragraph about two centimetres from the margin or leave a line to make it clear to the reader that you are introducing a new idea.

## How do I start?

If it is any consolation, this is the hardest task for *any* writer, not just students. The introductory paragraph is very important and MUST contain two elements:

1. Your interpretation of the question

2. A brief introduction to the main argument or ideas which follow

**The shape of an essay**

Just like the bones of a skeleton, the topic sentences in each paragraph must relate to each other in an organised way to form a shape. If they don't, the reader won't be able to follow your train of thought.

**How do I finish?**

Remember that your concluding paragraph sets the final impression of your work in the reader's mind. It should:

1. Summarise the main points of the essay.

2. Draw a conclusion which refers back to the wording of the first paragraph and/or the title.

3. Where appropriate, express a personal response to the question.

Try to think of the framework of an essay like this:

INTRODUCTORY PARAGRAPH

PARAGRAPH 1

PARAGRAPH 2

PARAGRAPH 3
and so on

CONCLUDING PARAGRAPH

## Linking paragraphs

In order to demonstrate a clear development of ideas, paragraphs should be linked and lead from one to another.  There are many useful signpost words and phrases which lead the reader through the essay and which make it easier to follow, such as:

- however
- it is necessary to consider
- but
- furthermore
- in conclusion
- yet

- on the other hand
- although
- another important point is
- finally
- therefore
- to sum up

## THE STAGES OF WRITING

### 1.  How do I plan?

If you are writing your essay for homework or as part of your coursework, you will have time to research and plan carefully.  It is well worth spending time on this stage of your essay as it will make the final process of writing much easier and your essay will have greater depth.

If you are writing your essay in an examination you need to make a quick plan before you begin to write. See Chapter 10, *Examination Technique*.

After completing the background reading you may feel overwhelmed by all the information floating around in your head. Don't panic – there are ways to gain control of your ideas and harness them.

a) **KEY POINTS:** When reading for information jot down key points on an A4 pad. Leave a wide margin so that you can add information later, and write on one side of the paper only.

b) Use Post-it notes to **BOOKMARK** vital pages in your reference books and always note page numbers.

c) **BRAINSURF** your ideas onto a large sheet of paper. First jot down everything that comes into your head – you may discard some of these ideas later but that doesn't matter.

d) **SORT** your ideas into paragraphs. Either circle using coloured pens or write numbers next to each point.

e) **WORK OUT THE SHAPE OF YOUR ESSAY:** Either draw a Mind-Map or draw up a list of numbered points, one for each paragraph. Remember to keep paragraphs simple – a topic sentence followed by three or four supporting sentences. Again, Post-it notes are useful: write each paragraph topic on a separate note and then stick them onto a blank sheet in order.

## 2. The first draft

Make sure that you use your own words to show that you have understood the information. Do not reproduce your lesson notes or copy from a textbook. If you have access to a computer it is a good idea to type up your first draft as it is then easy to insert material or delete information without writing out your essay again.

If you don't have a computer, try writing each paragraph on separate sheets of A4 so that you can rearrange them. When you are happy with the order you can number the pages and insert linking words so that one paragraph leads easily into the next.

Double-space your first draft to make correction easier.

## 3. Correction of the first draft

The best way to do this is to read your essay aloud. This will help you hear where you have expressed yourself clumsily, repeated yourself or missed words out. You should also be able to hear where to put in punctuation marks. Remember to check for commas, full stops, colons, semi-colons and quotation marks (see *Appendix* 1).

Check also for spelling mistakes. Even the spell-checker on a computer won't identify homophones (unless you are using a read back program such as *Read&Write GOLD*[8]): homophones are words which sound the same but which are spelled differently e.g. *where/wear*. A list of common spelling errors and homophones can be found in *Appendix 2*.

Check for grammatical errors (see *Appendix 3*).

Then ask yourself these questions:

- Have I read the question properly?
- Have I answered the question?
- Have I answered all parts of the question?
- Have I supported my topic sentences with examples, explanations, statistics or quotations?
- Does my essay follow a logical development?
- Have I avoided repeating the same ideas?
- Have I written a satisfactory conclusion?
- What mark would I give this essay if I were the tutor/examiner?
- Can I improve it in any way?

## 4. Write out your essay in full

## 5. Correction of the final version

After a break, read through your final version, checking that you haven't missed out any words and that you have copied spellings and punctuation correctly. Attention to such details is most important. When checking spellings it can be helpful to read the essay backwards.

Remember: **plan - draft - check - write - check**

---

[8] *Read&Write GOLD* is a program which reads back as you type, either word by word or sentence by sentence. It is available from textHELP!®.

# WRITING CLEARLY

When writing an essay you should aim to express yourself simply and clearly. Many students make the mistake of thinking that advanced work requires a more complex type of writing. They strive for a sophisticated style that can result in imprecise, 'woolly' expressions.

Unfortunately, such writing often suggests imprecise, 'woolly' thinking! If you have planned your essay carefully, you should know what you want to say and you should say it in clear, unaffected language.

**Some tips to help you improve your writing style**

- Write in your own words - don't try to sound impressive.

- Write in Standard English, not as you would speak. Avoid slang and exaggeration.

- Avoid idioms, i.e. well-known phrases or sayings (e.g. "at grass-roots level"). These make your writing seem tired and unoriginal.

- Don't be over-wordy:
  – avoid repetition unless it is necessary for emphasis
  – look out for tautology, i.e. saying the same thing twice
  (e.g. 'a temporary loan', 'meet together')

- Avoid unnecessary jargon. If you use the technical terms of your subject make sure that you define them or use them in the correct context to show that you understand them. Make sure that you spell them correctly.

- Avoid using personal pronouns ('I' and 'We'); distance yourself from your subject unless you are asked to give a personal opinion.

- As a general rule avoid abbreviations (use 'for example' instead of 'e.g.') and contractions (use 'was not' instead of 'wasn't'). Check with your tutor. In particular, do not use 'etc.' at the end of a list – it suggests that you have run out of ideas.

- Write in complete sentences. Every sentence must contain at least one verb and express a complete thought. Vary the length of your sentences to hold your reader's attention. In particular, avoid run-on sentences – linking two sentences with a comma or 'and'. (For more help see *Appendix 3*).

- Wherever possible, use direct statements.  Avoid expressions such as "It is considered that" or "It is the generally accepted view that" which suggest that you are afraid of expressing your own ideas.  For example, the statement

*"The Battle of Britain was considered to be a turning point in the Second World War."*

can be written more simply as:

*"The Battle of Britain was a turning point in the Second World War."*

However, the use of the passive voice is the accepted convention of scientific prose when you are writing up investigations or experiments:

*The experiment was conducted at normal temperature and pressure.*

- One of the best ways to improve your writing style is to read good prose.  Try reading a quality newspaper, especially the feature articles and the editorials.

***************

Remembering these tips, try re-writing the passage below:

Albert Einstein was an absolutely amazing mathematician, in fact the most amazing mathematician to date this present century.  His incredible theory of relativity broke new ground and really altered people's ideas and concepts about the nature of the universe.  He is considered to have changed people's ideas about time and space even though his theories are hard to understand.  As a young man in Switzerland he was soon on the road to solving his problems by means of mathematical calculations and in 1905 he published his first startling theory which went some way towards solving his problems and ten years later he completed the full theory of relativity.  Since Einstein first put forward his theory it has stood the test of time by many scientists and it is now generally believed that he was virtually a unique genius.

Look for examples of:

- run-on sentences
- slang
- exaggeration
- repetition
- indirect statement
- idiom
- tautology

The passage on the previous page contains 138 words. How many words are there in your version? You should be able to reduce the paragraph to no more than 100 words. (See *Appendix 4* for an example).

## SUMMARY

- **Interpret the question accurately by focusing on key words**
- **Plan your essay before you write the first draft**
- **Structure your ideas into a framework of linked paragraphs**
- **Check carefully by reading aloud**
- **Write in clear, formal English**

# CHAPTER 7

# COURSEWORK AND PORTFOLIOS

## Coursework

- **Define the task**
- **Time management**
- **Quality not quantity**

## Portfolios

- **Organising the portfolio**
- **Time organisation**
- **Working independently**

## COURSEWORK

At GCSE this has largely been replaced by controlled assessments, conducted under supervision.  However, it remains a component for some Level 2 and 3 courses post-16, such as BTEC, NVQ and some AS/A levels.  You may also find that the more vocational courses post-16 will include functional or key skills, including communication, application of number and information technology as these skills are vital to the world of work and further and higher education.

The amount of coursework and the type of external assessment depends on the awarding body.  You can find out more from their websites:

- AQA:       www.aqa.org.uk
- Edexcel:   www.edexcel.org.uk
- OCR:       www.ocr.org.uk

For those who do not give of their best in examinations, coursework can appear a welcome option.  You can work at your own pace; there is a much reduced demand placed on memory, and redrafting can take place over a period of time.  The coursework component can be worth as much as 30% of the final mark for some courses.  However, there are a number of pitfalls and great care must be taken in the preparation and execution of this component.

## DEFINE THE TASK

It may be that you can determine the title or subject matter.  This is not quite as easy as it may seem. It is important that you work very closely with your subject teacher when choosing this option.  The project must fit into the overall context of the course; it should display the specific skills being examined by the course and yet it needs to be manageable and not take a disproportionate amount of your time to complete. The exact requirements of the project need checking carefully and these can be found in the syllabus description for the subject being studied.

## TIME MANAGEMENT

The importance of good time management cannot be emphasised sufficiently. It is possible that you will be given as much as two or three months to complete a piece of coursework. Some teachers will give interim deadlines for separate components of the project, but very often only the final cut-off date is given. If this is the case, plan deadlines for yourself.

It could look something like this:

Week 1    Check reading list; buy or borrow suggested reading; order books from the library.

Week 2    Photocopy relevant sections; Start reading & highlighting key information. Start compiling bibliography. Surf the net.

Week 3    Prepare & distribute questionnaire/arrange to interview 'expert'/book visit to factory, business, studio, gallery, or whatever is relevant to the topic. Continue background reading; mark text with Post-it notes.

Week 4    Make detailed plan for coursework. Seek advice from teacher. Collect in questionnaire/write up visit or interview.

Week 5    Start writing (even if background reading is not complete). Write the introduction. Explain what you intend to do in the coursework. Describe research strategies.
Work on computer for ease of editing, or write on one side of paper only, & leave large right-hand margin for additional notes.

Week 6    Continue reading, writing and editing.
Interpret data, draw diagrams, mount pictures, etc.

Week 7    Complete the writing/diagrams etc.

Week 8    Leave the assignment for a few days, and then read again with fresh eyes. Complete the final editing.

## QUALITY NOT QUANTITY

It must be kept in mind that the quality of the investigation and recording/ writing must be carried out at advanced level standard, as the quality of the written communication is part of the assessment. The main criticism regarding coursework from the examiners is that it is often sloppily written and poorly structured. 'More' does not necessarily equal 'better'. Waffle and padding will be spotted immediately and needs to be avoided. Be clear from the outset how many words are required. All the points made in Chapter 6, *Essay Writing* with regard to interpreting the question, planning, organising and writing, apply to coursework.

## ORGANISING THE PORTFOLIO OF EVIDENCE

The evidence required for the portfolio can be produced in many forms, such as: written reports and notes; diaries or logs; photographs and drawings; recordings of interviews; questionnaires and graphic presentation of data; and possibly models and design work. You must file your work in an organised way right from the beginning. It is a good idea to have a large lever-arch file divided into sections or separate A4 files for each unit. Make sure that you date all your work and that you make a note of all references and sources. When working on the computer, save work regularly and remember to **back up everything**.

Your portfolio must be well presented and contain materials which demonstrate that you have completed the single assessment item for each unit of internally assessed work. You will be aware of the statements of what you must cover in each item in order to achieve grade levels E, C or A.

Your portfolio must be indexed and where evidence is included to support more than one unit or one of the Key Skills it must be duplicated or carefully cross-referenced. This can be achieved by using highlighters, symbols or coloured sticky labels.

**Two of the biggest challenges facing students after GCSE courses are organising their time in order to meet deadlines and working independently.**

## TIME ORGANISATION

This has already been discussed in Chapter 3, *Organisation and Time Management*. you must be able to set your own time frames for the completion of work.

It is important to get on with assignments as soon as they are set and not let the work build up. In particular, do not leave the important things until last.

Your tutor will give you a course outline or calendar. Transfer this onto a large wall planner in your bedroom or a personal organiser, alongside important deadlines for other subjects or other elements of your course, so that you can get an overview of all your commitments. Remember that the other subjects you may be studying will also have a coursework requirement with their own deadlines.

Secondly, you will be encouraged to keep a diary or record book of all your activities related to the advanced studies. If you mark the important deadlines in this diary in colour it will also help you remember when assignments are due. It is helpful to keep your diary up-to-date by making notes on a daily basis before you forget what you have achieved.

Note down everything you have done such as dates of presentations, times of interviews, meetings with guest speakers, and whether the outcome was a success. This will help you with the completion of your assessed units.

Advanced studies courses encourage good organisational skills. The following pointers may be helpful:

1. Break down everything into **small, manageable steps**.

2. When you are planning, **work backward from the deadline** and work out when each item needs to be completed.

3. **Set clear targets** when planning the steps needed to reach a particular goal.

4. **Review your progress frequently** to make sure that you are on track. You can do this by linking up with another student on the same course and monitoring each other's progress.


**If you stick to your plan you will never fail to meet a deadline.**


## WORKING INDEPENDENTLY

You will be expected to take far more responsibility for your own learning than when you were preparing for GCSE. In order to do this you need to develop self-awareness, to understand **how** you work and to know your own strengths and weaknesses (see the section on Learning Styles in Chapter 2, *Memory and Learning*).

You will also be expected to work with others on the completion of your assignments, as teamwork is an important aspect. Think about how you relate to others in a work situation and how you can best contribute to a group. Are you a natural leader?  Are you good at involving others? Are you better at practical tasks?  Remember that working as part of a team can now be assessed as a **Key Skill.**

Although you will be expected to work independently, this does not mean that you should not seek advice from your tutor.  Portfolios are very different from any work you will have done before and you will need support, especially at the beginning while you are adjusting and getting used to the system and the terminology.  Tutors are there to help.  They will not 'spoon feed' you but they will be able to give you assistance with the planning of internally assessed units and also provide you with an important sounding board for your ideas.

## SUMMARY

- **Organise your work carefully**
- **Log everything you do**
- **Remember – stick to your plan**
- **Consult your tutor – which is what s/he is for!**

CHAPTER 8

# INFORMATION AND COMMUNICATION TECHNOLOGY

- **Word processing**
- **Data display**
- **Research**
- **Note-making**
- **Electronic aids**

The aim of this chapter is to give an overview of the uses to which ICT can be put and to supply some addresses so that students can follow-up areas of particular interest.  To recommend specific hardware and software in this chapter would be of limited value as equipment and programs quickly become out-of-date.  Newspaper supplements often review the latest innovations and there are numerous specialist magazines.  ICT teachers and technicians at schools and colleges can prove an invaluable source of information and practical help.

## WORD PROCESSING

An obvious use for computers is the typing of projects and essays.

**Advantages:**

- Legible presentation
- Spell checker
- Thesaurus
- Grammar checker
- Word count
- Ease of editing
- Facility to insert tables, diagrams and illustrations
- A talkback program can help with proof-reading for punctuation
- Voice-recognition software is being constantly improved and is a viable option for those who cannot type or who type very slowly

**Disadvantages:**

- Problem of availability if you do not have your own computer
- Need to type at least as fast as you write
- Need to have at least a basic understanding of how to use a computer
- Need to be organised in saving and storing files for easy access
- Need for good proof-reading skills if using a voice-recognition program

If you are not accustomed to typing your essays and projects, you would be advised to give serious consideration to this mode of presentation if you aim to pursue higher education, as some university lecturers will not accept handwritten scripts. Discuss your needs with the ICT personnel at your school/college. You may be able to attend a class to learn word-processing skills or have access to a teach-yourself computer generated program.

## DATA DISPLAY

Professionally produced spread sheets, graphs, diagrams and illustrations can be created faster on a computer than by hand. In addition, once the initial data has been entered, it can be displayed in a variety of ways. Colour and three-dimensional effects can be included. However, check with your teachers as some courses require hand-drawn graphs for assessment purposes.

Photographs that you have taken on a field trip can be uploaded from your digital camera, smartphone or tablet for inclusion in your coursework. Printed documents such as newspaper articles and older photographs can be scanned and uploaded.

Timetables and daily schedules can be set up on a computer, smartphone or tablet and updated as necessary. This could be particularly useful if you were to note how you intend to use your study periods each week. Audible reminders in the form of an alarm can be programmed into your computer, smartphone or tablet to remind you of particular appointments and deadlines. These reminders/appointments can be synchronised between devices keeping you up-to-date wherever you are.

## RESEARCH

Research and information gathering can be carried out either by using the internet or, when necessary, older CD-Roms. The range of information available on the internet grows daily, which is both an advantage and a disadvantage. It is a disadvantage in that it can take a long time to track down what you are looking for, and it is very easy to become side-tracked by something that interests you, but is not relevant to your current work. Also the information may not always be accurate. It is essential to have anti-virus software and, whenever possible, try to obtain the web address of a site that covers the relevant topic before you start surfing. Ask your teacher or consult newspaper IT supplements which can be a useful source of information. Look at the names of websites before clicking on links to avoid arriving at an inappropriate site.

## NOTE-MAKING

Transferring notes that you have made in class or from your reading onto a computer has a number of advantages:

- **Review**

As mentioned in Chapters 2 and 9, if you can look through your notes within twenty-four hours, a week later and then a month later, it is possible to transfer a high percentage of new knowledge into long-term memory. Typing up your rough notes gives you the opportunity to revise the subject, and it also acts as a check on whether you still understand what you have written. If this is carried out whilst the subject is still fresh in your mind, you will stand a better chance of making good quality notes that you can draw on at a future date. Many tablets and handheld computers have facilities for electronic note-making that can be transferred to other machines for editing and revision purposes.

- **Legibility**

The notes can be re-ordered, spaced out, headings entered in colour, key words highlighted in bold print, and different fonts used for emphasis. The layout can be changed; points can be numbered; interrelating details can be displayed as a flow chart; and linear notes can be converted into a Mind-Map. There are some good programs available.

- **Additions**

Further information can be inserted into the notes as your background reading increases, this avoids having a collection of disjointed notes on the same topic.

- **Search facility**

By using the 'Find' facility on a computer it is possible to access information on a given topic that you have included in various sets of notes.

ICT

## ELECTRONIC AIDS

### Electronic Spell-checkers

If you do not have access to the spell-checker on a computer a hand-held spell-checker can save a great deal of time when proof-reading.  In order to check a spelling using a conventional dictionary it is necessary to know at least the first three letters to stand a chance of finding the word.  With an electronic spell-checker often it is possible to access the correct word even when an error has been made near the beginning of the word.  However, it is necessary to be able to recognise the correct word when scrolling through a suggested list of possible spellings.

Franklin produce basic spell-checkers, a thesaurus version so that you can investigate alternative words to make your writing more interesting, and a full electronic dictionary for definitions and roots.  Ensure your spell-checker is based on an English dictionary.

### Smartphones, handheld PCs and tablets

There are a growing number of applications to support reading, spelling, maths skills and organisation. Some have spell-checkers, voice to text and text to voice software built into the device.  It is also possible to use the camera function on some phones or tablets to photograph and enlarge text.  Optical Character Recognition (OCR) enables images to be converted to text files which can be read back.

A recent development is the availability of on-line rental services for school and college textbooks so they can be downloaded to a computer or e-reader and the files will self delete when the rental expires.  It is then possible to use the accessibility functions described above.

## REFERENCES

**iANSYST Ltd**
Web: **www.dyslexic.com**  Tel: 01223 420101  Information on talkback, voice-activated and mind-mapping programs, plus many other programs and aids.

**Texthelp Ltd**
Web: **www.texthelp.com**  Tel: 028 9442 8105  Information on BrowseAloud; Read&Write GOLD and other software solutions.

**Franklin Ltd**
Web: **uk.franklineurope.com**/products/spellers/  Tel: 01628 770988
Information on a range of spellcheckers and digital text readers.

## SUMMARY

- **Using word processing skills**
- **Develop techniques for checking your work**
- **Keep up to date with available technology**

ICT

# CHAPTER 9

# REVISION

- **Self-appraisal**
- **When to start**
- **What to revise**
- **How to revise**
- **A revision timetable**
- **Self-monitoring**

## SELF-APPRAISAL

How do you normally revise for tests and examinations?
Do your revision techniques work?

| Tick *yes* or *no* for the strategies you have used in the past, and for which strategies would be useful to try in the future. *Did you / would you:-* | Past | | Future | |
|---|---|---|---|---|
| | Yes | No | Yes | No |
| Read through your notes? | | | | |
| Copy out your notes? | | | | |
| Re-write your notes? | | | | |
| Reduce your notes? | | | | |
| Go back to your textbooks and start from scratch? | | | | |
| Highlight key words? | | | | |
| Underline headings and subheadings in colour? | | | | |
| Chant lists or text aloud? | | | | |
| Make an audio record of questions and answers? | | | | |
| Have question and answer sessions with your friends? | | | | |
| Draw pictures/Mind-Maps/flow charts? | | | | |
| Practise past papers? | | | | |
| Plan answers to past questions? | | | | |

Revision

If you found some strategies more helpful than others, why do you think this was so?  Jot down your ideas below.

…………………………………………………………………………………………………………..………

…………………………………………………………………………………………………………..………

Is there some link between what you have written above and your preferred learning style?     Yes / No

Comments: ………………………………………………………………………………...…………

Which of these strategies would you use in the future?

………………………………………………………………………………………………………

………………………………………………………………………………………………………

If you merely read through your notes, did you find that your mind wandered and you became bored quite quickly?  If you just learned your notes, but didn't practise past papers, did you find that when you came to take your exams you couldn't understand the questions, or that you didn't know how to match what you knew to the questions being asked?

It is important that you are aware of what works for you.  It is also important to assess which exercises prepare you for your exams.

If you used only one or two of the strategies listed above, experiment with the other suggestions to see which are effective.

There is one strategy in the table that you shouldn't need to use if you have accumulated appropriate notes – it should not be necessary to return to your original texts.  If you find you are doing this, re-read Chapter 5, *Taking and Making Notes* and ensure that in future you make notes from which you can revise.

## WHEN TO START

Students often ask when a revision programme should start.  The answer to this is not very popular with students.  Revision should start on the first day of the course!  "Impossible!" you may well cry.  "There is too much else to do".

However, the following points need to be kept in mind:

- If you do not review new work within twenty-four hours of a lesson, 80% will be forgotten (see Chapter 2, *Memory and Learning*).

- To appreciate a course fully, new work needs to be learned as you go along.
- Revision leading up to an exam should be concerned with reviewing (not learning from scratch) and practising sample questions.
- Modules throughout a course mean that there isn't just one main revision period at the end of a course. Revision needs to be ongoing.

Ongoing revision need not take too much time. Try the following:

- Within twenty-four hours of a lesson, read through your notes quickly. (You will bring your re-call up to 100%.)
- Underline headings in colour and highlight keywords.
- Check with friends if any of your notes don't make sense; rewrite where necessary.
- Add any new subject-specific words to a vocabulary notebook. Check on definitions (see example at fig.1).
- Ask someone to test you on the vocabulary already listed in the notebook.
- File the notes appropriately (you need to be able to find them again).
- When preparing for a class test, reduce long notes to shorter notes, or to a different format (see Chapter 5, *Taking and Making Notes*).
- As a topic is developed, add new keywords to a Mind-Map based on that topic. Pin it on your bedroom wall. Look at it before going to bed each night.

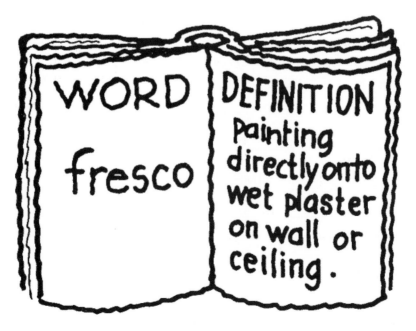

*Fig.1*

## WHAT TO REVISE

As you progress through the Key Stages you will find that courses are increasingly focused on interpreting, applying and evaluating new knowledge rather than regurgitating facts that have been learned off by heart. This is why an important part of any revision programme should be taken up with practising past papers. However, it is important that the tools of the trade are acquired, and so new subject-specific words, theories, principles and procedures need to be understood and learned. Subject-specific dictionaries are available for many subjects, but it is still useful to build up your own notebooks as you work through a course (see fig.1). Self-monitoring can be carried out by ticking off entries as they are learned.

Having an overview of the course is important. It is probable that your teachers will have given you a course syllabus. If they haven't, ask for one. This needs to be presented in a format that will be helpful to you so that you can monitor how much of the course has been covered, and how much is still to come. It will allow you to keep a check on how much you have revised and what you still need to work at. This may be a linear list of main topics and subtopics, or a Mind-Map (see example, Chapter 3, *Organisation and Time Management*).

Having an overview of your course will help you to prioritise what needs to be revised. When you have a class test, modular exam or end-of-course exam coming up, you need to decide what is essential, what is important, and what can be re-visited if there is time. Drawing yourself a priority mountain (see fig.2) or writing a bullet-point list, will give focus to your revision and help you to avoid wasting time.

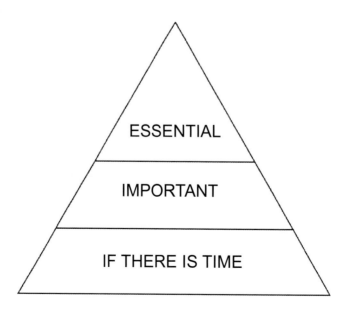

*Fig. 2*

**Take class tests seriously**. They are set to help you keep up-to-date with your ongoing revision programme. Your teachers will test your knowledge and understanding of topics highly relevant to your courses.

## HOW TO REVISE

With the insight you will have gained through analysing your results in the Learning Styles Questionnaire (see Chapter 2, *Memory and Learning*) you should have some awareness of how you learn best. Focus on strategies that suit your learning style whilst trying other approaches to enhance your learning potential. Here is a reminder of pro-active strategies that will help you to work efficiently, to keep focused and on task, and will help keep boredom at bay.

| ◆<br>**VISUAL, LEFT-BRAINED LEARNER** | ♠<br>**VISUAL, RIGHT-BRAINED LEARNER** |
|---|---|
| • Re-write notes using topic phrases and bullet points<br><br>• Underline headings in colour<br><br>• Highlight keywords<br><br>• Use mnemonics[9] and acrostics[10] | • Convert notes into Mind-Maps<br><br>• Convert notes into cartoon strip pictures<br><br>• Use colour and highlighting<br><br>• Convert notes into flow charts |
| ♣<br>**AUDITORY LEARNER** | ♥<br>**KINAESTHETIC/TACTILE LEARNER** |
| • Read notes aloud<br><br>• Record notes, quotations, questions and answers<br><br>• Discuss topics with friends<br><br>• Explain a topic to someone else<br><br>• Listen to recordings of set books and plays | • Write and draw images<br><br>• Practise experiments<br><br>• Handle equipment<br><br>• Act out scenarios<br><br>• Pace about whilst reciting information<br><br>• Use interactive revision programs or websites |

**Try to work in a multi-sensory[11] way by employing strategies from each box to fully utilise your brain and maximise your learning potential.**

---

[9] Memory aid: Richard of York gave battle in vain = colours of rainbow: R = red, O = orange etc.
[10] Memory aid: first letter of each word in a sentence spells a word: Sally Ann is dirty = SAID
[11] Using a number of the senses: hearing, seeing, speaking, touching.

# REVISION TIMETABLE

If you are given study leave before your exams it is important to plan your time carefully. You may find it helpful to use the following procedure:

- List the subjects to be revised.
- List the topics to be revised for each subject.
- Number the topics in each list in the order of importance. (Leave the most familiar topics till last.)
- Draw up a daily schedule, including what and when you will study. Use a weekly timetable (see the example in *Appendix* 5). Rule up each day according to the number of work sessions you plan. Don't forget to build in regular breaks (see fig. 3 below). Complete the timetable for the whole week and then assess whether you have shared out the time equally between your subjects, or whether you have allowed more time for the topics you enjoy most!
- At the end of each day appraise what you have achieved. Tick topics you have revised and make a note of any that will need re-visiting.

There will be some days when you won't be able to keep to your timetable, but don't let this make you abandon the whole plan. Transfer the sessions you have missed to an alternate time or the following week.

| REVISION TIMETABLE | | | | | | | | | |
|---|---|---|---|---|---|---|---|---|---|
| Mon | MATHS | B | GEOGRAPHY | L | Walk the dog | BUSINESS STUDIES | S | Read around subject |
| Tues | BUSINESS STUDIES | R | MATHS | U | Swim | GEOGRAPHY | U | Test |
| Wed | MATHS | E | BUSINESS STUDIES | N | Shopping | GEOGRAPHY | P | Read Geog. magazine |
| Thur | GEOGRAPHY | A | Driving lesson | C | Tennis | MATHS | P | BUSINESS STUDIES |
| Fri | MATHS | K | BUSINESS STUDIES | H | Walk | GEOGRAPHY | E | Cinema |
| Sat | BUSINESS STUDIES | | GEOGRAPHY | | Shopping | MATHS | R | Club |
| Sun | LIE IN | | GEOGRAPHY | | Watch film | BUSINESS STUDIES | | MATHS |

*Fig.3*

Under each subject heading, you would need to note which topic you intend to revise. Note that regular breaks and exercise are built into the timetable.

## SELF-MONITORING

It is important that you constantly reappraise how effectively you are revising. Try some of the following procedures:

- When revising a topic, write yourself some questions to test recall or understanding. After a break, or the following day, test yourself.
- Explain a topic to someone else. Did they understand?
- Make plans for sample questions.
- Record class test results. If you have a bad result, make sure you revise that topic again, even if you are not going to be re-tested in class as you may need the information for an exam.
- If you are struggling with your revision because your notes are inadequate or you do not understand a topic, consult subject-specific revision books, such as those published by Letts or Longman, and ask for help from your teachers.

## SUMMARY

- **Review your work regularly**
- **Learn new concepts and vocabulary as you go along**
- **Ensure your notes are clear enough for revision purposes**
- **Have an overview of your course/s**
- **Practise past papers**
- **Use a revision timetable for study weeks**
- **Appraise your progress**

Revision

# CHAPTER 10

# EXAMINATION TECHNIQUE

- **The run-up to the exams**
- **The night before**
- **On the day**
- **After the exam**

## THE RUN-UP TO THE EXAMS

If you have followed the advice given in Chapter 9, **Revision** during the weeks before the exams you should be able to approach them with some confidence. Avoid last minute panic by keeping to your revision timetable and obtain copies of past papers to work through.  It is worth studying the instructions on the paper carefully.  Ask yourself:

- How long is the paper?
- Is the paper divided into sections?
- How many questions do you have to answer?
- Are there any compulsory questions?
- Do some questions carry more marks than others?
- How much time do you have for each question?

Practise answering questions against a time limit.  Make sure that you allow time for reading the paper thoroughly and for checking at the end.

## THE NIGHT BEFORE

Even if you have not finished all your revision, don't study into the small hours on the night before an exam.  Stop working well before bedtime so that you get off to sleep quickly and wake refreshed.

Check that you have all the equipment you need and anything else such as tissues and your watch.

Check the time of the exam and the room in which it is to be held.  Make sure that your transport arrangements are secure and that your alarm clock is working!

Examination Technique

## ON THE DAY

**Stay calm**.
This is easier said than done!  If you have revised thoroughly you might even be looking forward to the opportunity to show what you know.  If you feel nervous, ask yourself what is the worst thing that could happen to you should you fail and what you could do about it.  Tell yourself that you can always resit, repeat the year or take a year out to rethink your future plans (see Chapter 12, **What Next?**).  Failing an exam is not the worst thing that could happen to you, so try to keep a sense of proportion.

Avoid talking to other candidates on the way to the exam.  You're bound to end up feeling that they know more than you do or have spent longer revising.  Remember that panic is infectious.  Instead, try to focus on what you are going to do once the exam is over.  If you must revise on the journey, concentrate on the mnemonics you have learned to remember key facts.  Keep them in your short-term memory so that you can jot them down as soon as the exam starts.

Breathe deeply and use the relaxation techniques outlined in Chapter 11, **Dealing With Stress**.

## In the examination room

Make sure that you are physically comfortable. If, for example, you are sitting in a draught or your desk wobbles tell the invigilator before the start of the exam. Check that you can see a clock and that you have registered correctly the time that the exam finishes.

Ignore everyone else.

As soon as the exam has started, write down any information, such as mnemonics, which you have stored in your short-term memory. This will reduce the demands on your working memory during the exam.

**Read the instructions on the paper carefully**. These are usually at the beginning but there may be some at the start of each new section of the paper. Check how many questions you have to answer and then spend time reading ALL the questions carefully. Guard against the temptation to start answering the first question you come across on a topic which you have revised. It may be that the wording is not as straightforward as that of some other questions on the paper. Don't fall into the trap of picking a short question because it involves less reading.

Ask yourself:

- What is the question actually asking?
- What should be included in the answer?
- What precisely is the examiner looking for in the answer?

**Interpreting the question correctly.** This is very important. Don't alter a question to suit what you know or have revised. Look carefully at key question words such as *describe* and *explain* and distinguish between them (see the list in Chapter 6, ***Essay Writing***). Underline or highlight the key words.

Make a careful selection of the questions you feel able to answer. Avoid those questions that might reveal inadequate knowledge of the subject or those that you don't really understand.

**Plan your time allocation carefully.** Jot down the time at which you will stop answering each question. Allow time at the end for checking. For your first answer choose the easiest question or one about which you know plenty. This will make you feel more confident and ease you into the paper. However, be careful not to spend too much time on the first answer, especially if you know a lot about it.

**Plan your answers carefully.** This will enable you to structure your answer and to avoid wandering off the subject. Brainsurf all the information you have stored on the subject and jot down key words. Re-read the question and cross out anything that you have written which is irrelevant. Now number the points in the order in which you will include them in your answer and cross them out as you write. Re-read the question again. Have you covered all aspects of the question in your plan?

In the opening paragraph of your answer explain your interpretation of the question. The first sentence should rephrase the question in your own words.

**QUESTION:** *"Women are less likely to commit crimes than men." Discuss.*

**ANSWER:** *Any discussion of the levels of crime committed by the male and female populations in this country must take into account . . .*

If the question requires short answers plan a sentence in your head before you write it, making it as concise as possible. If you are writing essay answers keep an eye on the clock. If you start to run out of time jot down notes or a plan of the answer that you would have written. You may get some credit for doing this.

**What should you do if . . .**

- your mind goes blank?
- you realise half-way through answering a question that you have misinterpreted it?
- you can't answer any of the questions?

1. If your mind goes blank it is because your stress level is very high. Take a deep breath and talk yourself through the panic. Think back to the room in which you had your lessons. Think back to the room in which you revised, to the music you were playing or to the colours you used to highlight your notes. The chances are that you will trigger off some response. If all else fails, start writing – anything – such as your name and address, to break the tension and reboot your memory.

2. There is nothing worse than the sickening realisation, halfway through writing an answer, that you have misinterpreted the question. If you have time start again and finish, if necessary, in note form. If you do not have time to start again finish the answer you are writing as this will leave a better impression than stopping halfway. You may not be penalised too heavily, especially if you have included some relevant information.

3. If you really cannot answer any of the questions, stay calm and take a deep breath. Remind yourself of the worst case scenario you rehearsed before. You probably can answer one or more questions; they may just be worded awkwardly. Reread the questions carefully. If you really cannot attempt any of them see if you can answer part of a question in order to show some knowledge of the subject.

**Concluding an answer.** When writing an essay answer it is important to summarise your response briefly at the end, referring back to the keywords in the question. This helps to convince the examiner that your answer has been relevant. Obviously you should not spend too long on this, especially if you are under time pressure.

**Checking.** Don't spend time checking until you have finished all your answers. Leave space between each answer so that you can add anything you may have missed out. Then read through your answers twice, paying attention first to meaning and then spelling, punctuation and grammar (see *Appendices 1, 2 and 3*). When reading for sense make sure that you have expressed your ideas as clearly as possible and have not contradicted yourself. Finally, make sure that you have entered all the information required on the front page of the answer booklet.

## AFTER THE EXAM

- DON'T hold a post-mortem with others. It will only depress you.
- Put the exam behind you. The results are months away.
- DO reward yourself by doing something entirely frivolous – such as going shopping – before preparing for your next exam.

### Postscript

It is worth remembering that examiners – the people who set and mark the papers – are human beings who want candidates to pass rather than fail. Try to imagine the examiner who will be marking your paper. S/he will most probably be an experienced or retired school teacher. Ask yourself what is likely to create a good impression apart from a knowledge of the subject. Pay attention to your style of writing and presentation. It is always difficult to write neatly when working under timed conditions but if you have untidy handwriting, practise writing on alternate lines of the paper. This will give a neater appearance to your work.

Examination Technique

**SUMMARY**

**Before the exam**
- **Research past papers**
- **Organise equipment the night before**

**During the exam**
- **Read instructions carefully**
- **Stay calm**
- **Check your work if you have time**
- **Reward yourself afterwards**

# CHAPTER 11

# DEALING WITH STRESS

- **Reasons for anxiety**
- **Symptoms of stress**
- **How to deal with stress**
- **Relaxation techniques**

Everyone feels stressed at some point during his or her advanced studies. The first thing to remember is that being stressed is a normal reaction to a demanding situation. When we feel nervous we secrete certain hormones which heighten our awareness and make us more alert. This reaction to stress has enabled the human race to survive from prehistoric times to the present day. It enabled cavemen to hunt successfully and to flee from predators. It is important to recognise that we are liable to feel anxious from time to time and to know how to deal with such feelings in order to avoid becoming over-anxious.

## REASONS FOR ANXIETY

Stress usually results from a combination of factors. For example, if you are having problems out of school or college you are less likely to deal with problems arising from your studies with a clear head. Try to identify exactly what is causing you to feel anxious and face up to it.

The most common causes of stress resulting from study are:

1. Feeling that you cannot cope with the demands of a course.

2. Feeling that you cannot cope with the total demands of two, three or even five courses; that you have taken on too much.

3. Feeling overwhelmed by the workload as a particular deadline approaches.

4. Feeling that other people are coping and that you are not.

5. Being surrounded by other students who are panicking which makes you feel edgy.

6. Worrying about the future. What should you do next? Will you get the grades you need? Have you chosen the right course in Higher Education? What will happen if you fail?

7.  Other people's expectations.  Teachers and parents can put students under considerable pressure – from the best of motives!  Schools are more concerned about the publication of performance tables than they have been in the past and parents worry because they want their offspring to achieve their potential.

8.  Your own expectations.  At this stage of your life your own self-image is based on several factors, one of which is your academic performance  Probably you have not yet had a chance to prove your capabilities outside the academic environment so your idea of your personal worth is likely to be based in part on your success at school or college.

If you throw into the melting pot all the other aspects of your life that might be worrying you, such as relationships, finances, or family tensions, it is clear that this is a stressful time in most students' lives.  Many people have commented that they found university far less demanding, so take heart!

## 1.  Feeling that you cannot cope with the demands of a course

This is a common reaction to Advanced Level study.  If you feel like this at the beginning of your course then it is likely that you are finding the transition to advanced level study daunting.  Look back at Chapter 1, *Introduction to Advanced Study Skills*.  As you get into your stride you should find it easier. If you continue to have difficulty, explain the situation to your subject tutor who can then advise you.  If you decide to change course, consider very carefully before you act.  You may well feel more comfortable with your studies after the first term.

## 2.  Feeling that you have taken on too much

Advanced Level study involves a considerable amount of background reading and research.  You may well feel that you are having to juggle the demands of several courses with all your other commitments.  Sometimes you feel so overwhelmed that your mind shuts down and you feel incapable of doing anything! When that happens it is a good idea to take a break and explain to your tutors how you feel.  They are likely to be sympathetic and to suggest strategies that will enable you to cope.  It may be that your teachers can see that your combination of subjects is too much for you and you can then consider alternatives.  Consider also whether the problem lies with your own lack of organisation see Chapter 3, *Organisation and Time Management*.

## 3.  Feeling overwhelmed as a deadline approaches

Again speak to your tutor.  If you have a genuine reason for not being able to meet a deadline most tutors will grant you an extension.  Often that is all you need: the feeling that you have one or two extra weeks to complete an assignment enables you to relax and recharge your mental batteries. You will then be able to settle down to work more efficiently.  If there are other reasons why you are falling behind try to analyse why this might be.  Do you fully understand the assignment?  Again, take advice.  If external pressures are preventing you from working, seek the advice of parents or other professionals such as your doctor.  You will feel better for talking about the problem.

## 4.  Feeling that other people are coping and that you are not

Are they *really* coping or is it your perception of the situation because you are worrying?  If there is someone in your group who is getting good marks when you are struggling, speak to him or her.  Ask if you can borrow an essay and compare it with yours.  S/he will be flattered and may well give you some useful tips.

## 5.  Being surrounded by people who are panicking

Seek out friends who are doing a different course.  Try to distance yourself from people who are making you feel stressed unless you feel that you can help them.

## 6.  Worrying about the future

This particular anxiety goes hand in hand with the fear of failure.  Our society lays great emphasis on being successful at a young age and this can put enormous pressure on young people.

Ask yourself what is the worst thing that could happen to you.  Mentally rehearse the worst case scenario.  So you have failed *all* your exams.  What will you do?  Resit?  Take a gap year?  Go to a college and take a one-year course to top up your points?  Then ask yourself whether in the long run it will really affect the course of your life.  Many successful people left school with very few academic qualifications and because they did not automatically go on to university they were able to take advantage of other opportunities which presented themselves.  Failure is *not* the worst thing that can happen to you.  Once you have accepted this it is easier to get things in proportion.

When choosing a course and checking that you are likely to get sufficient points for entry into Higher Education or a career, take advice from your Higher Education Advisor at school or college and ask for an interview with the Careers Advisor.  Make sure that you are fully informed about all the possible options.

## 7.  Other people's expectations

a) Teachers are realists and are unlikely to pressure you unless they feel you have the ability to perform.  So remember that if a particular teacher is demanding a higher level of performance it is probably because s/he feels that you are under-achieving.  Speak to the teacher about this if it is worrying you.

b) When it comes to parents, try to put yourself in their position.  They want the best for you and are bound to be disappointed if they see you going out clubbing midweek or lazing around all weekend.  When you are working, make it obvious to them.  If you feel that they are putting you under undue pressure (and sometimes parents are guilty of this, especially if they did not achieve at school themselves or if they have been very successful), try talking about how you feel.  Enlist the support of a teacher who might be able to explain tactfully what you can realistically be expected to achieve. It is always better to have your parents as allies.  Often they just need to be brought into the picture.

## 8.  Your own expectations

Be kind to yourself! Many students, especially if they have already achieved highly in the past, set themselves impossibly high standards and then feel that they have failed if they do not succeed in reaching them.  Set yourself realistic goals and make sure that you have interests in life other than academic work. If you enjoy playing a sport, do not give it up as exams approach.  Even if you are not very academic you are likely to be good at something. Be aware of your strengths and try to build on them.

## SYMPTOMS OF STRESS

There may be times when stress builds up to the point where it affects you physically and mentally.  Symptoms include:

- bursting into tears for no apparent reason
- mood swings
- outbursts of temper
- being unduly argumentative
- feeling very tired
- difficulty getting to sleep
- waking early
- feeling isolated or feeling sorry for yourself
- feeling angry with yourself
- headaches
- loss of appetite
- stomach upsets/diarrhoea

## HOW TO DEAL WITH STRESS

The best way to get things back into perspective is to tell someone about your feelings. Speak to your friends, your parents or your teachers.  If you are suffering from physical symptoms on a regular basis, go to see your doctor (don't forget that your doctor has had to study and take exams so s/he is likely to be very sympathetic).

- **Prioritise**. Ask yourself what really has got to be done, what can be left out and what can be left until a later date.  Make a list.
- **Don't work constantly**.  Take regular breaks.  You can justify these by reminding yourself that taking a break from studying enables the brain to consolidate new information.
- **Get some fresh air**.  Go for a walk or take some form of exercise.
- **Look after yourself**. Make sure you are eating properly.  Don't start to skip meals or graze.  Share mealtimes with other members of your household.  If you know that your diet is lacking, take a course of multivitamins.  Cut down on strong coffee and tea, alcohol and smoking.
- **Don't give up your social life**.  Going out every night is probably not a good idea, but meeting friends at the weekend will help you to keep a sense of proportion.

- **Reward yourself.** After a period of study, unwind in the bath, listen to music, go shopping.

## RELAXATION TECHNIQUES

**Try some of the following relaxation techniques:**

**Enjoy Aromatherapy oils in a burner**, in your bath or for a massage. They are easily available ready mixed in a carrier oil. Some blends will help you to relax, whilst others will wake you up and help you to concentrate. Lavender is particularly calming and can help you to sleep. Always read the instructions carefully as some essential oils should not be used if you are pregnant; if you intend to expose your skin to the sun immediately after a massage, or if you suffer from certain medical conditions.

**Take up Yoga**. You may not have time to join a local class, but watching a yoga DVD would demonstrate some ways of relaxing.

**Try other forms of exercise** such as **Tai Chi, www.taichifinder.co.uk** is a useful link to find out about classes and resources.

**Hypnotherapy** is another alternative therapy that can give benefit, especially if you are finding it difficult to concentrate. As there is no national organisation or professional body of practitioners it would be wise to consult your GP before trying this. Some GP practices have doctors trained in this technique.

You need to find out what works for you.

# MUSCLE RELAXATION TECHNIQUE

1. Lean back in your chair and stretch out your legs in front of you, or lie on the floor or on your bed.

2. Close your eyes. Concentrate on each part of your body as you tense your muscles.

3. First, curl up your toes. Tense the muscles in your calves, stretch your legs as hard as you can.

4. Hold that position and clench your hands into fists whilst stretching your arms out straight with your hands resting on your thighs.

5. Hold both positions. Feel the tension. Now bring your shoulders up to your ears.

6. Push your tongue to the roof of your mouth, frown and clench your jaw.

7. Feel the tension in all of your body. Count to 5: 1-2-3-4-5 and then let everything go.

8. Concentrate on feeling like a rag doll, all floppy.

9. Still with your eyes closed, imagine yourself lying on a sandy beach; feel the sun warming your skin; listen to the sea gently lapping at your feet. RELAX.

10. Slowly count down from 5: 5--4--3--2--1 and wake up.

11. Alternatively, let yourself drift off to sleep.

Dealing
with Stress

85

**REMEMBER** – if you are feeling anxious or stressed, you are not the only person to have felt like this. **TALK ABOUT IT**, as soon as possible. If you do not feel that you can approach anyone you know ring:

**ChildLine 0800 1111**, **www.childline.org.uk**
or
**The Samaritans 08457 909090**, **www.samaritans.org.uk**

## SUMMARY

- **Feeling stressed is a normal reaction**
- **Try to analyse why you are feeling anxious**
- **Take control of the situation**
- **Talk to someone**
- **Look after yourself**

# CHAPTER 12

# WHAT NEXT?

- **The options**
- **Taking advice**
- **Choosing a course**
- **Choosing a university**
- **Higher education and disability**
- **Money matters**

It is probably best not to start thinking about the future for the first half term of KS5. You will be busy enough getting into your new courses. As mentioned in Chapter 1, *Introduction to Advanced Study Skills*, this can be quite a heart-searching time deciding whether you have made the right choices and getting to grips with the new demands. Wait until you are established in your new routine before you start thinking about where your courses might lead.

## THE OPTIONS

After A levels or BTEC courses there are three main options:

- Straight into a job
- A gap year
- Further/Higher education

### Straight into a job

You may wish to experience the workplace before you decide whether further study would be appropriate. Often occupations are combined with planned training and lead to a National Vocational Qualification (NVQ).

A **Higher Apprenticeship** would lead to a NVQ at Level 4. An **Advanced Apprenticeship** would lead to a NVQ at Level 3 and an **Intermediate Apprenticeship** would lead to a NVQ Level 2. (Level 4 is equivalent to a Higher National Diploma or degree.) Some large companies operate their own training programmes. Before going into a job straight from school it is important to explore the promotion possibilities. You need to be aware of whether you will need formal qualifications at some point if you are to maximise your prospects.

## Applying for a job

Often you will be asked to send a **CV** (curriculum vitae) with a letter of application. This will detail your personal details, qualifications and experience. A suggested layout is included in *Appendix 6*. You may need to write a letter of application, some companies will specify in their advertisement that this should be hand-written, otherwise you can word-process the letter so that you can spell-check it. If you are going to write the letter by hand (a fountain pen looks best – you can buy inexpensive disposable fountain pens) it can be helpful to draft the letter first for ease of editing and then copy it out. Some or all of the following points will need to be included:

- Why you are applying for the job
- Why you think you would be suitable
- Previous experience that is relevant
- Your aspirations

Often, vacancies are not advertised and so you may need to send speculative letters asking for information about employment and stating what skills you could offer the company. There is more information at:

**www.4you.co.uk** – Jobs 4 you section
**www.apprenticeships.org**
**www.notgoingtouni.co.uk**

## A gap year

There are both advantages and disadvantages to taking a year out before embarking on higher education.

The advantages include:

A refreshing break from formal study

- The opportunity to mature and become more independent
- Time to travel
- Time to consider what you really want to do
- Time to save money for your future course

Disadvantages include:

Getting out of the habit of studying

- The expense – not all activities are salaried, in fact you may have to pay to do them
- Prolonging the time before you are qualified and start work

It is possible to take a gap year having been awarded a place at university on deferred entry. However, not all universities operate this system, or it may depend on the course you wish to take. Whereas it can be a positive advantage for some careers, for example, teaching, it is not always thought advisable for maths or the sciences, as you may get out of the way of problem solving. It is important to check whether deferred entry is an option at the colleges for which you are applying. Some colleges may expect your gap year to be spent gaining experience related to the course you intend to follow. Rather than applying for deferred entry, you may prefer to wait until after you have your exam results before applying for a course for the following year. However, you must ensure that you are available at the time applications have to be filled in and submitted, and for interviews.

If you have decided on a year out the following websites could be of use:

**www.raleighinternational.org**    **www.gap.org.uk**

**www.world-challenge.co.uk**    **www.bunac.org.uk**

These websites list the names of many organisations that provide both voluntary and paid work. They also detail all of the important and practical issues that need considering. They are unanimous in their advice to plan well ahead. Alternatively, if you would like a course that includes a year abroad consult *Erasmus* - **www.britishcouncil.org/erasmus**

## Further/higher education

The third option is to continue in education by taking a vocational course such as construction, or studying for a Higher National Diploma (HND), Diploma of Higher Education (Dip HE), Foundation Degree, or a full degree. Entry requirements for an HND or Dip HE are not as high as for a degree but on completion it is often possible to transfer to a degree course.

## TAKING ADVICE

Your school may provide a careers education programme starting in Year 8 or Year 9 that will help you develop knowledge, confidence and skills to make a well-informed, considered decision about your future plans to ensure that you progress smoothly into further learning or work both now and in the future.

However, some young people need extra help to make those decisions and would benefit from a one to one discussion with a Careers Adviser. You should speak to your school or college who will provide support and advice to help you. The National Careers Service offers information and professional advice about education, training and work to people of all ages. You can access support online, by web chat or by telephone. They can be contacted on:

0800 100 900 or at **https://nationalcareersservice.direct.gov.uk**

## CHOOSING A COURSE

When choosing a course you will need to compare the course content as it can differ widely between institutions. Other considerations include the teaching style – lectures, seminars, tutorials; assessment methods – yearly exams, continuous assessment, coursework. Discuss the implications with your teachers and current university students.

The UCAS website is a useful place to start your investigations as this has links to all universities, **www.ucas.com** There are also many publications available.

When considering where various courses might lead, a useful website is **https://nationalcareersservice.direct.gov.uk** which offers advice on careers and work choices.

*Choosing Your Degree Course and University* by Brian Heap, (Trotman Publishing) is essential reading and will be found in most local reference libraries.

Also by Brian Heap is *University Degree Course Offers: The Essential Guide to Winning your place at University*. This lists courses alphabetically and gives the grades that would be required; it also lists courses according to predicted grades.

Alternatively see *The Times Good University Guide* (updated annually). which incorporates the *Times University League Table* (published Times Books).

Much more information is available at:

**www.ucas.ac.uk**          **www.prospects.ac.uk**

**www.unistats.direct.gov.uk**          **www.ukcoursefinder.com**

## CHOOSING A UNIVERSITY

After conducting your preliminary research into courses and universities, you will need to draw up a short list of approximately twelve universities to consider more closely. Do not be overly influenced by the glossy pictures of abseiling or the jazz night. Initially, it is the course content you should consider, as this can differ markedly between one university and another.You must be confident that the course covers what you want to study. It may be necessary to take advice from your teachers or careers adviser regarding this.

Look at prospectuses in the careers library with the aim of reducing your choice to about six or seven universities. It could be as few as four. You may then wish to obtain your own copies of these prospectuses so that you can keep returning to the information for closer scrutiny.

*The Virgin Alternative Guide to British Universities* offers, as the title suggests, the kind of information not contained in prospectuses or official guide books.

Before accepting your firm and insurance offers it is important to have visited the universities. This can be at any time and need not be on an official Open Day. If you are to follow a technical course you need to ensure that the department is well resourced and up-to-date. It is also important to remember that, once you have accepted a university place, that is where you are going to live for at least the next three years. It is important that you are happy with the type of student, the facilities, activities and local town or city.

Photocopiable checklists are included in *Appendix 7* to help you record and compare information from several prospectuses.

## The UCAS form – selling yourself

The admissions tutor at the university will probably not spend more than two minutes looking at your application form and so it is important that your **Personal Statement**, in particular, is clear and concise, and sells you well. You will need to include some, if not all, of the following:

- Why you are applying for the course.
- Why you chose your advanced level courses – what you are enjoying about them – how they have given you an insight into the world of work or anything else that will display an enthusiasm for the subject/s.
- What work experience/leadership training or experience you have had.
- Your interests/hobbies. How you could contribute to the life of the university.
- Other skills.

You are likely to be submitting your application on-line. Write your Personal Statement in Word and import it into your UCAS application form. University and course codes will be inserted automatically by the system.

For further information see *How to Complete Your UCAS Application* published by Trotman.

UCAS forms need to be submitted by early January at the latest but it is advisable to send it as early as possible as some universities begin processing applications from the middle of October.

## Art Courses

If you have taken A level courses in Art and Design it is usual to take an Art Foundation Course before embarking on a degree. Your local colleges will supply you with information.

If you are already on an Art Foundation Course or a BTEC Level 3 Art and Design course there are two routes that can be followed.

The first follows the same procedure as for any other degree course and involves submitting a UCAS form between 1st September and 15th January. You can apply to a maximum of six courses.

Application forms for the second route should be sent to UCAS between 1st January and 24th March of the year in which you intend to begin the course. A maximum of three courses can be applied for and UCAS will send your forms to institutions sequentially according to your preferred order.

## The Performing Arts

If you wish to pursue a career as a performer in one of the arts (music, drama, dance) the following websites and sources will be of help:

UK Performance Industry: **www.ukperformingarts.co.uk**

Council for Dance Education and Training: **www.cdet.org.uk**

The Conference of Drama Schools: **www.drama.ac.uk**

The British and International Music Yearbook from **www.rhinegold.co.uk**

## HIGHER EDUCATION AND DISABILITY

If you have a disability the organisation Disability Rights UK publishes an annual guide, *Into Higher Education* which can be downloaded at:

**http://www.disabilityrightsuk.org/intohighereducation2013.htm**

It is available in both pdf and word formats.

Also, *Bridging the Gap: a guide to Disabled Students Allowances* can be downloaded from:

**www.direct.gov.uk**

**www.studentfinancedirect.gov.uk**

**www.studentfinancewales.co.uk**

**www.studentfinanceni.co.uk**

**www.saas.gov.uk (Scottish Awards Agency for Scotland)**

# MONEY MATTERS

Even if you think you will not qualify for financial support, it is important to investigate what grants are available. Your Local Education Authority will supply you with information regarding what grants you are entitled to and how much you can borrow through a student loan.

For detailed information and support go to the website:

**www.studentfinancedirect.gov.uk** which gives information on financial support for students and can be accessed by students and parents. The site offers guides which can be downloaded and application forms for loans and grants.

For details of non-government support, see *University Scholarships, Awards and Bursaries* by Brian Heap published by Trotman Publishing. Alternatively see: **www.support4learning.org.uk/money**.

This chapter has only scratched the surface of the issues surrounding '*The Next Step*'. Make good use of all the careers facilities at your school/college, and what you can find online, so that your decisions and plans for the future are well-informed.

**Good luck!**

# PUNCTUATION

Punctuation marks are like signposts to the reader.  They enable you to make sense of the text.  If they are omitted or used incorrectly they can obscure the meaning of what you have written.  When checking punctuation, work through this list in order.

1. **Capital letters** and **full stops** indicate the beginnings and endings of sentences.  Sentences are the building blocks of sensible prose and punctuation clearly indicates each unit of meaning.  In particular, avoid run-on sentences, that is two sentences separated by a comma instead of a full stop:

   *"Before a writer can begin he must have something significant to say, it is essential to research a topic effectively." (INCORRECT)*

   *"Before a writer can begin he must have something significant to say.  It is essential to research a topic effectively." (CORRECT)*

2. **Commas** indicate when to pause: these usually indicate endings of parts of complex sentences (clauses) and help the reader comprehend longer passages; commas also separate items in lists.

3. **Question marks.**

4. Avoid excessive use of **exclamation marks**!

5. Avoid using **contractions** such as *wasn't* unless you are comfortable with the apostrophe denoting a missing letter.  Contractions should not be used in formal writing.

6. Check the use of the **possessive apostrophe**:

   *the boy's books (books belonging to one boy)*
   *the boys' books (books belonging to more than one boy)*

   Remember: **it's** = it is; **its** = belonging to it.

   If in doubt about the use of an apostrophe, leave it out.

7. Make sure that you have introduced **inverted commas** (quotation marks) correctly, especially if you have used quotations.

### Punctuation of direct speech – examples

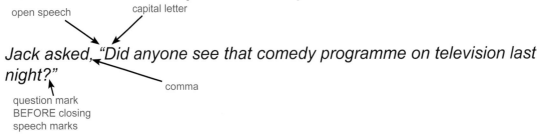

Jack asked, "Did anyone see that comedy programme on television last night?"

open speech
capital letter
comma
question mark BEFORE closing speech marks

"Did anyone," he asked, "see that comedy programme on television last night?"

small letter - not the beginning of a sentence

"Did anyone see that comedy programme on television last night?" he asked.

small letter - not the beginning of a sentence

"No, I missed it," she replied.

comma after an interjection

Single inverted commas to enclose a title within speech

"I watched 'The Comedy Show' last night," he announced.

### Punctuation of quotations and titles

When you are quoting directly from a source you must:

- introduce the quotation as part of the preceding sentence
- enclose the quotation in inverted commas
- keep to the original lines, especially when quoting from a literary source.

For example:

*In his later plays, such as 'The Tempest', Shakespeare expresses a philosophical acceptance of the transitory nature of human existence. This is evident in Prospero's speech in Act 4 when he declares,*

*"We are such stuff*
*As dreams are made on, and our little life*
*Is rounded with a sleep." (Act 4 Scene 1, lines 156 – 158)*

**Note:** that the title of the play is enclosed in single inverted commas, and how capital letters have been used.

8. Make sure that you use **colons** and **semi-colons** correctly. Otherwise leave them out.

   **Colons** are used to introduce a list or an explanation:

   *There are many examples of punctuation marks: commas, full stops, colons and semi-colons.*

   **Semi-colons** are also used to separate items in a list when the list contains phrases rather than single words. The list is introduced by a colon:

   *Over 2,000 years ago a Greek named Antipater of Sidon compiled a list of the Seven Wonders of the World: the Statue of Zeus at Olympia; the Temple of Artemis at Ephesus; the Colossus of Rhodes; the Pharos of Alexandria; the Mausoleum at Halicarnassus; the Pyramids and the Hanging Gardens of Babylon.*

   **Semi-colons** can also be used to link two main clauses which are closely related in meaning in a sentence instead of using and or but:

   *The team was well-trained; its victory well-earned.*

9. **Check paragraphs**. Start a new paragraph for each new topic and indent the beginning of the paragraph about two centimetres from the margin. Paragraphs make it easier for the reader to follow what you have written by breaking up the text on the page and by indicating that there is a change in meaning or a development of thought.

# SURVIVAL STRATEGIES FOR SPELLING

If you are a weak speller there is little point in trying to learn (or re-learn) spelling rules at this stage. Instead try some of the following strategies:

1. **Use a dictionary**. Find one with a clear layout that suits you. *The Oxford School Dictionary* leaves a clear space between each entry which makes scanning easier.

2. **Use an electronic spellchecker**. *Franklin* produce a good range of electronic dictionaries, some of which also contain a thesaurus, "soundslike" searching and speech output facilities. You do however have to be able to recognise the correct spelling from a list of options, (available from iANSYST).

3. **Use a word-processor** for homework and coursework and run the spell-check. However, this will not detect homophones, words which sound the same but which are spelled differently (unless you have a read back program like *Read&Write GOLD*). A list of some of the most commonly confused words can be found at the end of this section (see List 2).

4. **Keep a personal dictionary** of the errors you make in essays and coursework. Experience has shown that by correcting your three most common errors you can eliminate up to 50% of your mistakes.

5. **Learn commonly misspelled words** (see List 1) using the **Look-Say-Cover-Write-Check** method:

   **LOOK** at the correct spelling of the word. Notice any difficult parts.

   **SAY** the word aloud, pronouncing each part separately.

   **COVER** the word up and try to see it in your mind.

   **WRITE** the word, saying it as you write. Don't look back at the original word.

   **CHECK** your spelling against the correct version. Repeat the process if you have made a mistake.

6. **Concentrate on subject-specific words** and technical vocabulary when writing essays and in examinations. Keep these words with their definitions on index cards and file them alphabetically for reference or use a separate notebook.

7. If all else fails, **try bluffing**. Eileen Stirling stresses the importance of word beginnings. If you spell the first chunk of a word correctly a reader can often correctly surmise the rest even if it is incorrectly spelled by using the context of the sentence. Make sure that you are familiar with the spellings of common prefixes – a letter or a group of letters added to the beginning of a word which changes its meaning (see List 3).

8. **Revise the rules** for adding endings (suffixes) on to root words (see List 4).

## List 1 – Commonly Misspelled Words

| Word | How to remember its spelling |
|---|---|
| height | height |
| accommodate | 2x c, 2x m, 2x o |
| necessary | 1 collar and 2 socks |
| sincerely | sincerely |
| business | business |
| separate | separate ( a rat) |

# List 2 – Commonly Confused Words

**accept/except**
I **accept** the gift.
They all arrived **except** Jim.

**access/excess**
The **access** to the building was wide enough for wheelchairs.
An **excess** of sweets may lead to tooth decay.

**advice/advise**
It is not always easy to accept **advice**.
I **advise** you to drive carefully.

**affect/effect**
By expressing my opinion, I was able to **affect** the outcome of the meeting.
The **effect** of the painkillers was to make him feel drowsy.

**allowed/aloud**
You are not **allowed** to walk on the grass.
He spoke his thoughts **aloud**.

**board/bored**
He nailed a wooden **board** across the broken window.
She was **bored** during the lesson.

**bought/brought**
She **bought** a new dress for the party.
As there was room in the car I **brought** some friends.

**breath/breathe**
His **breath** steamed up the car's windscreen on the cold morning.
It is impossible to **breathe** underwater.

**cereal/serial**
My brother's favourite breakfast **cereal** is porridge.
I missed the last episode of the television **serial.**

**choose/chose**
Which book did you **choose** to take on holiday?
I **chose** a biography.

**council/counsel**
The Parish **Council** decided to improve the playing fields.
I accepted the **counsel** of the legal advisor.

**curb/kerb**
You must **curb** your anger.
He tripped up the **kerb**.

**clothes/cloths**
The **clothes** he was wearing were unsuitable for an interview.
Put the dish **cloths** under the sink.

**complement/compliment**
A **complement** is an amount which completes something e.g. the music complements her voice beautifully.
If you admire someone's dress, you pay them a **compliment.**

**decent/descent**
Her dress was too low-cut to be considered **decent**.
Their **descent** from the mountain summit was hindered by storms.

**desert/dessert**
The Sahara **desert** is full of sand.
Banoffee Pie is a sweet and sticky **dessert**.

**fair/fare**
I enjoy riding on the Ferris Wheel at the **fair**.
He did not have enough money for his bus **fare**.

**have/of**
I would **have** given anything for his autograph.
The basket **of** fruit looked very attractive.

**hear/here**
You **hear** with your ear.
Where is it? Over there? No! Over **here**!

**hole/whole**
Mind that **hole** in the pavement!
The **whole** school contributed to the fundraising event.

**knew/new**
I **knew** there was something wrong when I saw her face.
My **new** shoes were pinching my toes.

**know/no**
I **know** how to change a wheel on my car.
I have **no** money left at the end of the week.

**lay/lie**
"Will you please **lay** the table for me?"
**Lie** down and relax.

**lightening/lightning**
The combination of sunshine and seawater is **lightening** her hair.
The golfer was unfortunately struck by **lightning** on the seventh green.

**loose/lose**
The boy pulled out his **loose** tooth.
Don't **lose** it," said his mother. "You can put it under your pillow tonight."

**miner/minor**
The life of a coal **miner** is physically demanding.
The loss of a handkerchief is a **minor** problem.

**night/knight**
The longest **night** of the year comes just before Christmas.
The **knight** and his lady lived in the castle.

**passed/past**
The scrum half **passed** the ball to the inside centre.
He ran **past** the full back.

**peace/piece**
They longed for **peace** so that the soldiers could return home.
"May I have that last **piece** of cake?"

**practice/practise**
She could not attend the netball **practice** after school.
You must **practise** your backhand in order to improve your tennis playing.

**quiet/quite**
The puppy curled up in a **quiet** corner and fell asleep.
He was **quite** breathless after running after the bus.

**right/write/rite**
I often confuse left and **right** when giving directions.
You must **write** the date at the top of the page.
A **rite** is a ceremony which may have a religious purpose.

**their/there/they're**
They had forgotten **their** books.
Where? Over **there**!
**They're** three words which are easily confused. (they + are = they're)

**threw/through**
He **threw** the ball to the wicket keeper.
The ball sailed **through** the open window.

**where/ were /wear**
**Where** are you going?
**Were** you at the concert last week?
I have nothing to **wear** to the party!

**whether/weather**
Have you decided **whether** you are going or not?
The **weather** was unusually fine for the time of year.

**whose/who's**
**Whose** socks are these?
**Who's** going to the meeting? (who + is = who's)

**your/you're**
**Your** dinner is on the table.
**You're** going on holiday next week. (you + are = you're)

# List 3 – Common Prefixes

| prefix | meaning/origin | example |
|---|---|---|
| ab | from  (L.) | abstain |
| ad | to  (L.) | advance |
| ante | before  (L.) | ante-room |
| anti | against  (Gr.) | anti-social |
| auto | self  (Gr.) | autonomous |
| bi | two  (L.) | bicycle |
| circum | around  (L.) | circumvent |
| com (co) | with  (L.) | command |
| contra | against  (L.) | contra-flow |
| counter | against  (L., Fr.) | counter-attack |
| de | removing, down  (Fr.) | destroy |
| dis | not, apart  (L.) | disentangle |
| ex | out, away  (L.) | exhume |
| hyper | over, excessive  (Gr.) | hyperactive |
| in | in, into, towards  (L.) | invade |
| inter | between  (L.) | interrelate |
| mis (**not** miss) | badly, wrongly  (OE.) | misbehave |
| over | over, too  (OE.) | overreact |
| post | after  (L.) | post-operative |
| per | through  (L.) | percolate |
| pre | before  (L.) | premeditate |
| pro | for, in front of  (L.) | proceed |
| semi | half  (L.) | semicircle |
| sub | under  (L.) | subway |
| super | over, greater  (L.) | superstar |
| tele | far  (Gr.) | telephone |
| trans | across  (L.) | transport |
| tri | three  (L.) | tripod |
| un | not  (OE.) | unhappy |
| under | below, lower,  (OE.) | underneath |

Key
    L. = Latin; Gr. = Greek; Fr. = Old French; OE. = Old English

# List 4 – Adding endings (suffixes)

**VOWELS:** a e i o u, and y at the end of words
**CONSONANTS:** b c d f g h j k l m n p q r s t v w x y z

1.  When adding a suffix to a base word first look at the letter which starts the suffix. If it is a consonant, just **add** the suffix to the root word.

    **Consonant suffixes: s, ness, less, ful, ly, ment**

    > dog - dogs, sad - sadness, hope - hopeless

    > thank - thankful, glad - gladly, pay – payment

2.  If the suffix begins with a vowel you need to look at the ending of the base word.

    **Vowel suffixes: ing, er, ed, y, en, es, est, able, ous**

    If the base word consists of one syllable, with one vowel and one consonant after the vowel, you must **double** the final consonant when adding a vowel suffix:
    > stop, – sto**pp**ed, sto**pp**ing

3.  If the base word ends in an **e, drop the e** before adding a vowel suffix:
    make – making, confuse – confusable

    Exceptions to this rule are words which end in **ce** and **ge**:
    > notic**e**able, courage – courag**e**ous

4.  If the base word ends in a consonant, followed by a **y, change the y to an i** before adding a suffix:
    > happy – happ**i**ly, marry – marr**i**ed

5.  If the base word ends in a vowel, followed by a **y**, just **add** the suffix:
    > play – played, buy – buyer

6.  Words which end in **l**, double the **l** before adding a vowel suffix:
    > label – labe**ll**ed, labe**ll**ing

7.  Words which end in **ic, add** a **k** before adding a vowel suffix, to stop the **c** becoming a soft sound:
    > panic – panicking

# GRAMMAR

Many Advanced Level students will have received little formal teaching in English grammar, so what should you look for when checking your work?

1. You can often "hear" grammatical errors so whenever possible (not in exams!) read your work aloud. There are now computer programmes such as *Read&Write GOLD* available that will read back work which you have typed on the word-processor. This will enable you to detect where you have omitted words.

2. Look for agreement between the subject of the verb (the doer of the action) and the verb (the doing word). A singular subject must have a singular verb. For example, the statement,

    "We **was** looking for a solution" is incorrect; it should be
    "We **were** looking for a solution".

    People often make mistakes when there is more than one subject of the verb; for example,

    "My brothers and I **was** interested" should read
    "My brothers and I **were** interested".

3. When checking agreement make sure that you have spelled plural words correctly. It is very easy to leave off **s or es** when writing at speed. Some plural forms are irregular or derived from Latin; this is particularly true of technical words such as **formula/formulae; locus/loci.**

4. Check the tense of the verb and check that you have used it consistently. For example, if you are writing about events in the past you must use the past tense throughout. Have you put **ed** on the end of all the verbs which need it?

5. Have you written in proper sentences? A sentence is a group of words which makes complete sense and which contains at least one verb. Every simple sentence contains one finite (complete) verb and in a complex sentence so does every clause.
    For example:

    SIMPLE SENTENCE:      The children **ran** home from school.
    COMPLEX SENTENCE:   The children **ran** home from school
                                          because they **wanted** to see their new puppy.

A common mistake is to write a sentence which has only part of the verb, for example,

"The airport on a bank holiday was a nightmare scene. Everywhere, travellers **sprawling** across seats."

This second sentence should be,

"Everywhere, travellers **were sprawling** across seats."

6. Students often confuse the comparative and superlative forms of the adjective. Make sure that you know these irregular ones:

the **good** boy; the **better** student (out of two); the **best** pupil in the class

the **bad** girl; the **worse** student (out of two); the **worst** student in the school

# WRITING MODEL

(**See Chapter** 6, P.51)

Compare your version of the paragraph about Albert Einstein with the one below.

Albert Einstein was an outstanding mathematician of the twentieth century. His theory of relativity altered people's concepts of the nature of the universe, time and space, even though it is difficult to understand. In 1905, as a young man in Switzerland, he first published an early version of his theory based on mathematical calculations. Ten years later he completed the full theory of relativity. Since then it has been tested by many scientists and Einstein is now regarded as a genius. (81 words)

APPENDIX 5

# PLANNERS

## YEAR PLANNER

|    | AUG. | SEP. | OCT. | NOV. | DEC. | JAN. | FEB. | MAR. | APR. | MAY | JUN. | JUL. |
|----|------|------|------|------|------|------|------|------|------|-----|------|------|
| 1  |      |      |      |      |      |      |      |      |      |     |      |      |
| 2  |      |      |      |      |      |      |      |      |      |     |      |      |
| 3  |      |      |      |      |      |      |      |      |      |     |      |      |
| 4  |      |      |      |      |      |      |      |      |      |     |      |      |
| 5  |      |      |      |      |      |      |      |      |      |     |      |      |
| 6  |      |      |      |      |      |      |      |      |      |     |      |      |
| 7  |      |      |      |      |      |      |      |      |      |     |      |      |
| 8  |      |      |      |      |      |      |      |      |      |     |      |      |
| 9  |      |      |      |      |      |      |      |      |      |     |      |      |
| 10 |      |      |      |      |      |      |      |      |      |     |      |      |
| 11 |      |      |      |      |      |      |      |      |      |     |      |      |
| 12 |      |      |      |      |      |      |      |      |      |     |      |      |
| 13 |      |      |      |      |      |      |      |      |      |     |      |      |
| 14 |      |      |      |      |      |      |      |      |      |     |      |      |
| 15 |      |      |      |      |      |      |      |      |      |     |      |      |
| 16 |      |      |      |      |      |      |      |      |      |     |      |      |
| 17 |      |      |      |      |      |      |      |      |      |     |      |      |
| 18 |      |      |      |      |      |      |      |      |      |     |      |      |
| 19 |      |      |      |      |      |      |      |      |      |     |      |      |
| 20 |      |      |      |      |      |      |      |      |      |     |      |      |
| 21 |      |      |      |      |      |      |      |      |      |     |      |      |
| 22 |      |      |      |      |      |      |      |      |      |     |      |      |
| 23 |      |      |      |      |      |      |      |      |      |     |      |      |
| 24 |      |      |      |      |      |      |      |      |      |     |      |      |
| 25 |      |      |      |      |      |      |      |      |      |     |      |      |
| 26 |      |      |      |      |      |      |      |      |      |     |      |      |
| 27 |      |      |      |      |      |      |      |      |      |     |      |      |
| 28 |      |      |      |      |      |      |      |      |      |     |      |      |
| 29 |      |      |      |      |      |      |      |      |      |     |      |      |
| 30 |      |      |      |      |      |      |      |      |      |     |      |      |
| 31 |      |      |      |      |      |      |      |      |      |     |      |      |

This page may be photocopied for own use.

# DAILY PRIORITY LIST

**WEEK BEGINNING** ...................................................................

| MON. | ................................................................... | |
|------|-----|---|
| TUE. | ................................................................... | |
| WED. | ................................................................... | |
| THU. | ................................................................... | |
| FRI. | ................................................................... | |
| SAT. | ................................................................... | |
| SUN. | ................................................................... | |

This page may be photocopied for own use.

# TIMETABLE

**WEEK BEGINNING** ...................................................

(Rule up for required number of periods/breaks)

| | |
|---|---|
| MONDAY | |
| TUESDAY | |
| WEDNESDAY | |
| THURSDAY | |
| FRIDAY | |
| SATURDAY | |

# REVISION TIMETABLE

| | S U P P E R | | L U N C H | | B R E A K | |
|---|---|---|---|---|---|---|---|
| MON. | | | | | | | |
| TUE. | | | | | | | |
| WED. | | | | | | | |
| THU. | | | | | | | |
| FRI. | | | | | | | |
| SAT. | | | | | | | |
| SUN. | | | | | | | |

# WRITING A CURRICULUM VITAE (CV)

## NAME

Address

Tel.

E-mail

Date of Birth                           Nationality


### EDUCATION

name the most recent school/college first
list only secondary education

Start/finish date                name of college or school
A levels/AS/A2                  subjects (grades)
Start/finish date                name of college or school
GCSEs                              subjects (grades)


### WORK

name the most recent work experience first

Date(s)                            Company
(describe the nature of work)


### ACTIVITIES

In school                         e.g. sport, music, drama, clubs, etc.
mention any position of responsibility
e.g. team captain; editor of newspaper; etc.

Out of school                  e.g. St John's Ambulance; gospel choir; etc.


### ADDITIONAL SKILLS

e.g. driving licence; computer skills; first aid
training, etc.


### REFEREES

list at least 2 people
name, address, telephone number
e-mail address

# TIPS FOR WRITING YOUR CV

- Write on no more than two sheets of A4.
  Some employers will specify just one sheet.

- Use phrases, not sentences.

- Use the tab keys for consistent alignment.

- Use an interesting, but not fussy, font.

- Be consistent in the use of bold (e.g. just for sub-headings).

- Use bold in preference to underlining.

- Be as concise as possible;
  further detail about the relevance of work experience, for example, can be included in your letter of application that will accompany your CV.

- Print on good quality paper;
  its more likely to be noticed and will show that you have taken the trouble over your application.

- Check your spelling carefully.

# UNIVERSITY PROSPECTUS CHECKLIST

This checklist is for recording and comparing information on universities. There are more boxes overleaf so you can add additional information. You may wish to research the facilities for a particular disability, or you may be looking for a particular sport or society. If you are thinking of taking a GAP year, do check if you can defer your offer.

| UNIVERSITY | 1 | 2 | 3 | 4 | 5 |
|---|---|---|---|---|---|
| UCAS Code | | | | | |
| Course Title | | | | | |
| Prospectus page number | | | | | |
| UCAS course code | | | | | |
| Typical offer (grades/points) | | | | | |
| Phone number | | | | | |
| City/rural | | | | | |
| Accessibility (ease of travel) | | | | | |

# SEN Marketing

SEN Marketing is a specialist travelling bookshop. We sell books, games and equipment, including software, for children and young people with special educational needs. We specialise in providing materials for teachers and students with dyslexia; dyspraxia; ADHD; Aspergers; autism and speech and language difficulties.

Send for our latest catalogue to:

SEN Marketing
618 Leeds Road
Outwood
Wakefield   WF1 2LT

Tel/Fax:  01924 871697
E-mail:  sales@senbooks.co.uk
**www.senbooks.co.uk**

We visit many local and national exhibitions and conferences during the year, including Special Needs London and NASEN Live!
Please do call us and invite us to be the bookshop for your event.